Visiting in an Age
of Mission

OTHER WORKS BY KENNON L. CALLAHAN

Effective Church Finances

Effective Church Leadership

Giving and Stewardship in an Effective Church

Twelve Keys to an Effective Church

Twelve Keys: Audiocassette Tapes

Twelve Keys: The Leaders' Guide

Twelve Keys: The Planning Workbook

Twelve Keys: The Study Guide

Kennon L. Callahan

Visiting in an Age of Mission:

A HANDBOOK FOR PERSON-TO-PERSON MINISTRY

HarperSanFrancisco

A Division of HarperCollinsPublishers

Library of Congress Cataloging-in-Publication Data
Callahan, Kennon L.
  Visiting in an age of mission : a handbook for person-to-person
ministry / by Kennon L. Callahan.
    p. cm.
  ISBN 0–06–061287–8
  1. Visitations (Church work) 2. Lay ministry 3. Evangelistic work.
  I. Title
BV4320.C33 1994
253'.7—dc20   93–39488
                                                                  CIP

        96 97 98 ❖ RRD(H) 10 9 8 7 6 5 4 3 2

To Tom Shipp, Glen Johnson, Merle Weaver, and Olive Smith. Their grace and spirit, their compassion and hope have enriched our lives beyond measure.

Kennon and Julie Callahan

Contents

Acknowledgments

May this book benefit you. May grace, compassion, community, and hope be yours. May your life be enriched and your mission blessed.

I want to thank the many persons who have shared their lives with me. Their love and support mean much. From my earliest days as a pastor, visiting in the community has been central. Across the years, I have had the privilege of visiting with many people. I thank them for what they have taught me. This book is a testament to their contributions to my life.

I want especially to thank Julie McCoy Callahan. We've worked together on many books, and even more closely together on this book. Her insights have been most helpful in this work.

I want to thank John Shopp, senior editor at Harper San Francisco. He is a good friend with whom I've shared and worked for more than a decade. I greatly appreciate his wisdom and clarity. I'm also grateful for the team of people with whom I work at Harper San Francisco.

I want to express my thanks to D'Wayne Roberts, who typed the manuscript and contributed many excellent suggestions to the revisions that followed. She has shared good wisdom.

I have profound appreciation for all who have visited and are visiting in the name of Christ. May this book help you with your visiting and with your life. May the compassion and hope of God be with you.

Introduction

This book is for you, to help you grow your visiting. You will help people in the name of Christ.

Read the book with a spirit of joy. Be in prayer. You'll discover suggestions, wisdom, resources. Claim your competencies and develop them. Your life will be enriched.

Invite someone to study the book with you. Meet to discuss it, to pray, and to have fun. Share new insights and discoveries. You'll grow with one another.

God gives us an amazing mission. We can fulfill this mission when we visit with people in both our community and our church. The suggestions in this book will help

- those who visit
- evangelism and mission leaders
- pastors and staff
- denominational leaders
- new congregations
- renewing congregations

God invites us to visit with those in our community. This is precisely what mission congregations do. Institutions focus inside. Mission movements focus outside. In this age of mission, visiting is a crucial part of sharing God's joy and compassion.

STEP ONE:

The Persons

1:

A Joyful Invitation

THE INVITATION

Go. . . . *Matthew 28:19, Mark 16:15*

Welcome. God has given us one of the richest ages for mission the Christian movement has ever seen. Welcome to the first century. Welcome to the twenty-first century. We live in the time of the great invitation. Welcome to the best time of your life. Your life will make a difference for God's mission.

These steps will help you grow your visiting:

1. Discover those whom God is inviting you to visit.
   We will consider nine possible groupings of persons in your community.
2. Choose your ways of visiting.
   We will look at fourteen possibilities.
3. Decide the best timing.
   We will consider the best times of the year.
4. Grow your gifts for visiting.
   We will look at the ways you can enhance your strengths and competencies for visiting.

5. Build your mission. We will look at how you can develop
    a simple plan for visiting in your community.

Do these steps with the spirit of joy, the sense of caring,
the purpose of shepherding. Do them with the motivations
of compassion and community. God will bless your visiting.

MISSION

Visiting is mission. We're helping people with their lives and
destinies in the name of Christ. Visiting is evangelism. We're
helping persons discover God in their lives. Visiting is sacred. We go knowing we are sent by God, that we have been
given a sacred trust.

MINISTRY WITH REAL PEOPLE, NOT THE "UNCHURCHED"

Visiting is *with* persons. It is not *to* persons, where one talks
and the other listens. Nor is visiting *at* persons. We're not
trying to pressure, hassle, or hustle.

Our visits with persons are reciprocal—two-way, inclusive, participatory. Visiting is not vertical and top down. It is
horizontal and grassroots.

God sends us to visit with *individuals*, not some imper-
sonal grouping, not simply with the "unchurched." Now is
a good time to give up any preoccupation with this imper-
sonal category. We visit persons.

God's grace and compassion are shared with all people.
The very term *the unchurched* puts some at a disadvantaged,
one-down position. The biblical text is clear. John's gospel
doesn't say, "For God so loved people in churches." The good
news of the Gospels, compassionately and confidently, is

> For God so loved *the world,* that He gave His only be-
> gotten Son, that whoever believes in Him should not
> perish, but have eternal life. *John 3:16*

God invites us to help people with their lives and destinies. The term *unchurched* creates the impression that the primary goal of visiting is to get the unchurched churched. We have a higher calling than that.

God invites us to visit with persons in our community. We're not called to visit members only. We're invited to visit with *community persons*. This term affirms that we live together in the same community. It affirms that our visiting has to do with more than getting people churched.

To be sure, community persons are not members of a church. They don't participate in a congregation. That's fine. They are people for whom God has given us a mission. God encourages us to help them. As one wise, caring person once said, "We are put on earth to help one another."

When we visit, we are called to look for ways of helping. Our task is deeper, more helpful, than trying to move people from a category called "unchurched" to a category called "churched." God invites us to help people live rich, full, joyous lives in Christ.

Visiting is being a good friend in the name of Christ. In visiting it is never quite clear who is helping whom. Each shares and each receives. When our visits help bring forth the best in those we visit, we are being good neighbors.

Likewise our visiting allows others to bring forth the best in us; it allows them to be good neighbors too. Sometimes the person we are helping is in fact helping us to live our lives at our best.

A NEW DISCOVERY

For many, visiting with people in the community is a new discovery. Years ago, going to church was *the* thing to do. People sought out the church on their own initiative, willingly. Churches thought they had all they could do simply to keep up with the droves of new people finding their way to congregations during those years of a churched culture. As

a result, in some congregations—indeed, in some denominations—visiting with people in the community was virtually discontinued. It became a lost art.

Churches came to assume that people would find them.
Churches became preoccupied with pleasant programs and
busy committees. They found themselves trapped on a
merry-go-round, caught in a whirlwind of activities that
went faster and faster, blurred more and more as the years
went by. They deployed their leaders in a culture of committees. They lost the art of mission visiting. Their focus
turned *inside.*

Visiting is a genuine art. It's not simply a skill or an en-
terprise the church does to avoid dying. It is an art that
needs to be shared and practiced. When muscles are not
used, they atrophy and wither. Just so with the art of visiting. Unused, it fades away. There came a time in the culture when going to church was no longer the thing to do.
Virtually an entire generation missed the value and art of
visiting for mission. They lost the practice of visiting with
persons in the community. For people and pastors in congregations, it became a missing memory.

We need the *new* discovery of visiting with persons in
our community. Across the centuries of the Christian movement, people have always been busy. And, across these same
centuries, there has been a rich tradition of visiting.

Mission movements share visiting. Institutions hold
meetings. The church has never been at its best as an institution. The church has always been at its best as a mission
movement. As we move into the twenty-first century, we
are called to take on once more the shape and momentum
of the mission movement.

Mission movements visit as naturally as people
breathe, as regularly as the sun rises and sets. With mission
movements, visiting with community persons is in the very
fabric of their being. It is through visiting that they reach

out in sharing and shepherding ways to those in the community.

GO

Jesus shares with the disciples a joyful invitation,

>Go. . . . *Matthew 28:19, Mark 16:15*

They had lived through three extraordinary years. Having been called by Jesus, the disciples lived together with him during an amazing time. They heard the teachings. They saw the wonders and the miracles. They spent time apart with their Lord.

They had seen Christ share his compassion again and again. The people loved him and followed him. They had experienced the celebration of Palm Sunday. The kingdom was surely coming.

Then Golgotha smashed their hopes. Fear and doubt overcame them. Despair, depression, and despondency pressed in upon them. They hid for their lives.

Then they experienced an open tomb, the risen Lord, and new life in Christ. Easter came. The disciples began to understand more fully the nature of the kingdom.

The disciples were filled with joy. They were overflowing with excitement, laughter, and rejoicing. They were filled with good news—so much so that they were bursting with wonder and happiness. Jesus was smiling, laughing, sharing their joy. The three years had been worth it. The disciples finally did understand. Much was yet ahead, and they would do well.

It is as if Jesus, with a gentle smile, had said to the disciples,

>Go and share. Yes, you have my encouragement.
>You have my reassurance.

The great banquet has begun. The wedding feast is
    here. The kingdom has come.
Go with laughing wonder.
Go with tears of joy,
With the drenching rains of grace,
With the tumbling waters of good news.
Go and share the resurrection of compassion and
    hope. I will be with you.

"Go" is a joyful invitation, not a stern challenge. It is a
gentle encouragement, not a solemn command. Jesus was
not berating the disciples. He was not pushing and harass-
ing them. He was not detailing some new legalism. The
risen Lord was present with them. They were puzzling
through what they might do with this good news.

Jesus shared with them the joyful invitation, "Go." With
wonder and gladness we, like the disciples, can respond to
Christ's joyful invitation—and go.

2:

Choosing Whom
to Visit

When visiting is done in the right spirit, with the right intentions, people will find home in your visiting. Before you start the actual visiting, therefore, determine whom God is inviting you to visit. Discover your longings to help with specific human hurts and hopes. These guidelines will help you choose whom to visit first:

- Discover those whom you would have fun visiting, whom you could visit in a spirit of cheerfulness.
- Find out what your personal competencies and strengths are.
- Think about what you can offer to the community's, and the individual's, search for meaning, belonging, and hope in life.
- Demonstrate a sincere concern for another's well-being rather than getting sidetracked on church growth.

CHEERFULNESS

God loves a cheerful visitor. We are not pressed to visit out of duty or obligation. We are invited to visit with a cheerful joy and hopeful expectancy. We are called to visit with a confident, assured spirit—with a sense of celebration and good news.

In his second letter to the congregation at Corinth, Paul wrote,

> God loves a cheerful giver. *2 Corinthians 9:7*

Likewise I am confident God loves a cheerful visitor. We are called to visit with joy and wonder, with a lively, merry spirit.

We are the Easter people. We are the people of hope. We are the people of new life. The good news overwhelms us. The wonder of God's grace surrounds us. There is gaiety and laughter. The spirit is stirring and inspiring, warm and exciting. Our deepest yearnings and longings have been fulfilled in our risen Lord.

In the gospel according to Matthew, Jesus says,

> The kingdom of heaven may be compared to a king who gave a wedding feast for his son. *Matthew 22:2*

The kingdom is not compared to a solemn meeting or a somber program. The kingdom is not a place of boredom. It is not a dull, dreary event. It is a wedding feast. It is a time of great joy and celebration.

In the gospel according to Luke, Jesus says,

> A certain man was giving a great banquet, and he invited many. *Luke 14:16*

In both the Matthew text and the Luke text we discover that some who were invited did not come. Too much has been made of those invited guests who did not come.

In both texts the master sends his servants out to invite more guests.

> Go therefore to the main highways, and as many as
> you find there, invite to the wedding feast.
>
> *Matthew 22:9*

> Go out at once into the streets and lanes of the city
> and bring in here the poor and crippled and blind and
> lame. . . .
> Go out into the highways and along the hedges.
>
> *Luke 14:21, 23*

We learn three things: The kingdom is like a wedding feast, a great banquet. God is earnest in inviting people to the wedding feast. God encourages us to invite people to the kingdom.

Begin where you can best begin. As you select those you will be visiting, select first those you would have fun visiting. Think of your visiting as inviting guests to a wedding feast, a great banquet. Think of yourself as the Christmas people, the Easter people. In that joyful and celebrative sense, consider those you would have fun visiting.

When you share visits with a sense of joy and a spirit of fun, you will bless the lives of others. When you are glad to see people, people are glad to see you. There is a radiance, a transforming presence, in that kind of visiting. We are not called to be the people of doom and gloom. We are not called to be the people of sullen frowns and somber faces.

Rejoice! The Messiah has come. Rejoice! the Lord is risen. Rejoice! The Spirit leads us forward. Select those persons in your community with whom you can first and best share this joy.

COMPETENCIES

Consider your competencies. Don't try to do everything. Too much yields too little. Those who try to do too much in visiting end up doing too little. Without focus, they spread their visiting efforts among too many persons.

Start your visiting by selecting those in your community who match your competencies. You may feel competent in helping parents of preschool children. Perhaps you feel that your strengths lie in helping people who are in early retirement. Fine. Begin with them.

Think through the strengths with which God has blessed you. Do not choose persons that, for the moment, match your current weaknesses. Do not choose those you think you should, ought to, or must visit. Select *first* the persons in your community you can best visit.

THE SEARCH FOR VALUES

As you select persons you plan to visit, think through what would be of value in your community. Because visiting contributes to the community, there is a direct correlation between mission visiting and the character and quality of life in the community. The healthier the congregation's visiting in the community, the healthier the character and quality of life in the community. Healthy congregations have a healthy visiting relationship with the community.

In our time people are searching for

- individuality
- community
- meaning
- hope

The search is urgent and desperate. People long for and look for fulfillment in these life searches. As you visit with people, you can show your respect for their individuality—for their identity and integrity. And you can share your own spirit of individuality. You can help people with their low self-esteem and sense of powerlessness. You can help them deepen their sense of value and worth.

We all long for community. Feeling a sense of lostness and loneliness, we look for family and friends. The family networks that used to support people are scattered across the planet. We search for community, not committee. Your visiting is a way of sharing community. You offer a sense of roots, place, belonging.

As you visit, be aware of persons' search for meaning. We all want some sense of the value, significance, and purpose of our lives. The ways persons used to make sense of everyday life are not working as well today. Your visiting can help persons discover new meaning for their lives.

We all look for hope. Be aware of your own search for hope as well as that of the person you are visiting. Hope is stronger than memory. Wearied by too much alienation and depression, people crave sources of hope for their lives. They want to live beyond despair. They want to live with hope, and your visiting can help.

Through visiting, people advance and improve, families grow and develop, the community and the world become more helpful, healthful places in which to live. As you visit, you contribute to the character and quality of life in your community.

THE PROMISE OF MISSION VISITING

We live in a new world, in an age of mission where we can no longer count on social conformity to deliver new persons to our congregations. Focus on mission visiting and its promise.

The first step is to discover the persons you sense God is leading you to visit. Grow the spirit of mission as you select who you will visit. Try not to get caught up in visiting for the purpose of church growth. Don't visit primarily out of a concern to add to your membership. We can live beyond church growth. God calls us to grow the mission.

More is at stake in visiting than simply getting more members. At stake when we visit is helping people advance their lives and destinies in the name of Christ. We do the mission for the integrity of the mission.

Go with joy. Be a cheerful visitor. Do the mission well. God will bless it and your sharing.

3:

An Amazing Mission

PACE AND PROGRESS

God gives us an amazing mission. I encourage you to grow your visiting with a spirit of joy and celebration *and* a sense of pace and progress. This will build the strength of your mission.

As you select whom to visit, discerning your choices with wisdom and prayer, think about those you plan to visit in year one. At the same time look four years ahead. Having a vision for the future of your visiting will help you develop a sense of pace and will allow you to measure your achievements.

Enjoy your visiting. Be at peace. You can kill your enjoyment of visiting by trying to do too much too soon. You don't need to visit with everyone in year one.

Do your visiting well with one grouping of community persons in year one. You will build a self-generating, self-renewing mission with them. You'll see that it works, that it helps, and you'll find it easier to expand your visiting with new persons in subsequent years.

POSSIBILITIES

A mission field invites a focus on people in the community. Mission congregations visit with those in their communities. Institutional congregations focus within. Mission movements focus outside. I urge you to look forward to and to enjoy visiting with people in your community. Table 3.1 lists several examples of community persons with whom you might visit.

First-time worshipers are those who come to your congregation on a Sunday morning and participate in worship or church school for the first time. Yes, there are out-of-town visitors and visitors from other churches. First-time worshipers, as understood here, live in your community and don't currently have a church home. Visiting with them is a natural follow-through.

Newcomers are distinct from first-time worshipers. First-time worshipers may have lived in the community a long time; they have found us. Newcomers have recently moved into the community. Further, first-time worshipers have sought us out. Newcomers have moved into the community, and we are seeking them out.

One way to discover newcomers is to find out who is moving away. Someone new will move in where they lived, and the new arrivals provide you with a natural opportunity to visit. You can obtain deed-closing lists, a matter of pub-

Table 3.1 Community Visiting Possibilities

First-time worshipers	Relational persons
Newcomers	Specific vocational groupings
Occasional worshipers	Specific neighborhood groupings
Constituent families	Inactives
Persons served in mission	

lic record at the local court house. Real estate agents can advise you of new arrivals. Businesses will supply, for a fee, the names and addresses of newcomers in the community. You can explore the many listings available in most communities.

Occasional worshipers are community (nonmember) persons who worship with us now and then. Usually they are with us for Christmas, Easter, and other major community Sundays. Their occasional presence with us is their way of teaching us that if they did have a church home, it would be here with us.

Constituent families are community families with persons who participate in some church activity from time to time. Community families are nonmember families. I favor the term "community families" over "nonmember families." The former term is more missional and inclusive. The latter term is institutional and separating.

Persons served in mission are those in the community whom our congregation has helped in recent times with a specific human hurt and hope, with a life stage, with a wedding, a funeral, a hospital visit. They are nonmembers, nonconstituents. They do not belong, and they do not participate. At the same time, your congregation has recently helped them in some way.

Relational persons are community persons who have a relationship with someone in the congregation. They are acquaintances, work associates, friends, or family. They are part of the relational networks of people in your congregation.

Specific vocational groupings are community persons who engage in a given vocation. In our time, people live in what I call vocational villages. It is possible and reasonable for you to be in mission with a specific vocational grouping in your community.

Specific neighborhood groupings are community persons who live in a distinctive neighborhood area. You could focus on a specific geographical neighborhood within the average trip time of your congregation's location.

Inactives are those who were formerly active in your congregation. They are better understood as community persons than as church persons. Technically they do continue to be members. Practically, you can best relate to them and visit with them as community persons.

ORDER OF SIMPLICITY

These groupings have been listed in their order of simplicity. *First-time worshipers* and *newcomers* provide good opportunities to learn the art of visiting. First-time worshipers are already seeking us out. Their coming to church is not accidental; they have some purpose in mind.

Visiting with newcomers is a natural opportunity to welcome them as part of the community. Our purpose in visiting is not to try to get them to church. Welcoming them as part of the community is a generous, comparatively simple form of visiting.

Visiting with *occasional worshipers* and *constituent families* is a somewhat more advanced level of visiting. These persons are participating on occasion in worship or some grouping or program in your congregation.

Visiting with *persons served in mission* and *relational persons* invites progressively more visiting experience. They have a direct connection with your congregation, and, at the same time, they do not currently participate.

To share visits with *specific vocational groupings* or *specific neighborhood groupings* is for seasoned, experienced visitors. It makes good sense to visit with them, and yet you are beginning with fewer direct relationships. Visiting with *inactives* is best accomplished when you have gained much experience and wisdom through visiting. Visiting with inactive persons is worthwhile. At the same time, the best way to squelch the growth of your visiting is to begin by calling on inactives.

To use a sports analogy, visiting with first-time worshipers and newcomers is like playing junior high ball. Visiting with occasional worshipers and constituent families is like playing senior high ball. Visiting with persons served in mission and relational persons is like playing college ball. Visiting with a specific vocational grouping and a specific geographical neighborhood is like playing pro ball. Visiting with inactives is like playing super-pro ball.

The best way to grow your visiting experience is to begin at the beginning level. Then you can move forward to more challenging possibilities. Play junior high, senior high, college, and pro ball. Learn to visit with some of these community persons. Then grow your way forward to super-pro ball.

INACTIVES

Know these things about inactives. First, there is no such thing as an inactive person. Inactive persons are not waiting at home for us to find them. Inactive persons are, in fact, actively searching for a sense of community somewhere else, because—for whatever reason—they did not find it here with us. Second, for most inactives, something simple interrupted their pattern of participation, and no one noticed. Regrettably, we remember the few inactives who left in a huff, angry and upset. Most inactives simply slip away. They began to participate less frequently, and no one cared. They finally stopped coming altogether.

Third, a flexible rule of thumb is: For however many years they have been inactive, it will take that number of contacts to help them become active again. For a person who has been inactive for four years, it may take four visiting contacts to get the person back again.

SELECTION

Select one to four possibilities for community visiting over the next four years that match the guidelines outlined in chapter 2. In the beginning, set aside any preoccupation with inactives. Choose a good match for you personally from among the first eight possibilities. Later you can select other community persons as you grow your visiting.

Keep your focus limited. Your best way forward may be to focus on only one grouping, and that one may provide you with an excellent visiting mission. Some congregations have been so helpful with one grouping of community persons that they become legends on their community grapevines. The reason I suggest one to four is so that you will see that there is an outer limit. You don't need to do all nine.

Use your best wisdom. Be in prayer. Select well. Begin with one, and, for the moment, select no more than four possibilities for the visits you're planning during the coming four years. God will bless your mission.

Community Persons

_____

_____ First-time Worshipers

_____ Newcomers

_____ Occasional Worshipers

_____ Constituent Families

_____ Persons Served in Mission

_____ Relational Persons

_____ Specific Vocational Groupings

_____ Specific Neighborhood Groupings

_____ Inactives

Instructions: Select one to four groupings of community persons you look forward to visiting.

STEP TWO:

Ways of Visiting

4:

Visiting Possibilities

EVERYDAY LIFE

I encourage you to visit with persons in the same ways people ordinarily visit with one another. In everyday life people are in contact with one another in many ways. Indeed, we have developed a vast array of ways to communicate with one another.

There are many excellent possibilities. Select the persons in your community God is calling you to visit, and then choose the most helpful ways of visiting. There is more than one way to visit.

Visit the ways people normally visit with one another in everyday life. The Christian movement has always reached out to people using commonplace, natural means of communication—simple human sharing and conversation. Look anew at how people in your community share and visit with one another. These will likely be the most effective ways for you to be in contact with persons in the name of Christ.

EXCELLENT POSSIBILITIES

Certainly a home visit is among the most effective ways of visiting with people. At the same time, it's not the only way, nor, indeed, is it necessarily the most effective way. Listed in Tables 4.1, 4.2, and 4.3 are fourteen possibilities for visiting with persons.

Use your creativity to consider which of these fourteen possibilities will work best in your own visiting. Each is discussed in depth in the following chapters. Across the centuries, the Christian movement has shown considerable creativity in using the ways of visiting available at the time. The earliest mission efforts of the first century used

- home visits
- work visits
- personal notes
- personal letters
- small group gatherings

Table 4.1 Personal Visiting Possibilities

Home visits	Personal notes
Work visits	Personal letters
Personal phone calls	

Table 4.2 Possibilities for Visiting in Gatherings

Small group gatherings	Community events
Large group gatherings	

Table 4.3 Possibilities for Special Ways of Visiting

Direct Mail	Newsletters
Televisiting	Audio cassettes
Door invitations	Video cassettes

- large group gatherings
- community events

All of the available possibilities were used during that first age of mission. As new means of contact have emerged throughout the centuries, the Christian movement has included them. In our present age of mission, God has given us a wide range of possibilities.

TAILOR YOUR VISITS TO THE INDIVIDUAL

Look at the people you plan to visit in your first year. Consider one, two, or three ways of visiting that will be helpful in reaching out to them.

The art is not to single out only one way. The art is to choose whatever visiting possibilities

- correspond to the ways people normally visit with one another in your community
- suit the community persons you seek to help
- match your own competencies
- develop flexibility in the ways you seek to reach persons in the name of Christ

A classic mistake is to choose one method and run it into the ground. Because something worked well one time in one place, don't assume that it will work well for all time and in every place. No one way can automatically be used as *the* way everywhere, every time.

Each of the fourteen possibilities for visiting has its devotees. Some claim that one method is the most effective for them. The key words in that assertion are "for them." That way worked in a given context for a given time in a distinctive community. All fourteen possibilities, in fact, have worked well in a number of places over a period of time.

Any number of these possibilities have the potential to work well when you contact, for example, first-time worshipers. What takes wisdom is choosing the one to three ways that will be the most helpful, the most effective—with the specific first-time worshipers in your community in a given year. That is the art. No one possibility has a monopoly on helpfulness and effectiveness. Don't lock yourself unilaterally into just one.

Once you choose the one to three methods that would be helpful in reaching first-time worshipers, you don't automatically need to use the same methods later when visiting newcomers. You might decide that other ways would be more effective. And you can choose yet other ways when reaching out to relational persons.

Use your best wisdom and creativity, your best shepherding instincts, and rely on your finest recent experience.

MATCH VISITS WITH COMPETENCIES

Some people are effective with work visits, personal phone calls, and direct mail. Others do best with personal notes, door invitations, and newsletters. There are fourteen possibilities. Consider the ones that coincide with your competencies. Use those visiting possibilities.

Not everyone is good at home visits. Some are best at personal notes or in small group gatherings. Give thoughtful consideration to which you can best utilize.

It would be a mistake to focus primarily on the possibilities you would have time to do. Some people say, "I really don't have time to do such-and-such." Frequently what they mean is that they do not feel they have the necessary competencies for that way. Think about what you're good at. You'll find time to do those things that help you grow your strengths, gifts, and competencies.

DEVELOP FLEXIBILITY

Your visiting experiences will come alive when you're as flexible, creative, and imaginative as possible. You have chosen the visiting possibilities that best match

- the persons you are visiting
- your competencies

Now encourage flexibility and creativity in yourself. You don't need others to decide for you. Others can suggest; you decide. Discovering your own ways forward will energize your mission.

We have the confidence that God goes before us as a cloud by day and a fire by night, leading us toward the future that God has both promised and prepared. We have the confidence that we are the people of the risen Lord, the Easter people, the people of Christ.

We are the people of grace and compassion. We are not the people of legalism and law. We are not a top-down, unilateral, inflexible people. We have a firm confidence in a spirit of hope, in a sense of the future, in a vision of infinite potential. Mission movements live out a spirit of flexibility. Develop and live out your own flexibility. For example, some first-time worshipers might be contacted with a home visit, others with a personal phone call, or others with a personal note.

With some newcomers you might welcome them with a home visit. With others a personal phone call may be best. With some you might send a direct-mail invitation to an important community Sunday. Some relational community persons are best contacted with a personal note, through a personal phone call, a direct-mail invitation, or a combination of these.

Count on your flexibility, creativity, and imagination from one year to the next. You might decide that certain ways of visiting with relational persons will work best in a given year, and that another way will work well the second year. You might discover that you are more competent and comfortable with other possibilities.

Have a spirit of search and flexibility, of trial and error, from one year to the next. Develop a spirit of discovery about what is genuinely helpful when you visit. For centuries the Christian movement has had a remarkable ability to search out, discover, and adapt new ways to match with new times and new persons.

Be in a spirit of prayer. Invite God to lead you forward. Puzzle with wisdom and creativity the ways of visiting that will help you reach people in the name of Christ.

5:

Personal Visiting

This chapter explores five personal visiting possibilities, each putting you into some form of personal contact with others. Among these, the home visit is most significant.

HOME VISITS

It is better to be in persons' lives than in their living rooms. Some of the most helpful home visits are held on the front porch. They may last only several minutes. The purpose of home visits is not to get inside and spend time in the living room. The purpose is to begin a relationship with a person.

Use your creativity to discover the best ways to visit with persons in their homes. Don't try to achieve an idealized image of a home visit. You will probably not be gathering the whole family; you will not be sitting down in the living room having a pleasant chat for an hour to an hour and a half. People with an idealized image seldom do real visiting.

Some people work hard to find a wide range of semilegitimate excuses to avoid doing home visits. One of the most frequent excuses I hear is that no one is at home anymore. True. At the same time, a home visit is extraordinarily helpful and meaningful to people.

There is a sacramental significance in going to a person's home. You communicate your positive interest in their lives. Even when they are not at home, your presence—and the note you leave—will convey your genuine compassion for them. You have been willing to invest the time to visit with them in their home.

When they are not at home, do leave a note, not a church business card, which will only communicate an institutional, functional message. And do not write on a card, "Sorry I missed you." That is a double negative, "sorry" and "missed."

Point to what can be, rather than to what has not happened. A helpful message to write on a personal note when you are sharing, for example, a follow-up contact with a first-time worshiper is

Dear John and Mary,

Glad we could worship together this morning.
    I look forward to our visiting.
    I'll give you a phone call.

                              Yours,
                              Bill Freeman

This is a people-centered note.

Yes, a home visit can translate into a personal note when people are not at home. It may be followed by a personal phone call. Just know that people are helped immeasurably by a home visit.

WORK VISITS

I once consulted with the leaders of a dying church. Their former pastor had been there for sixteen long years. In a fresh, new way each Sunday over those sixteen years, that pastor had taught the congregation that they were a dying church.

He was in over his head and didn't know what to do. And he was ingratiating himself to the people. In effect he had been saying, "See how gracious and loyal I've been to stay with you all these years, even though you are a dying church."

Fortunately he retired before he killed the church.

We had gathered in the sanctuary with the new pastor to ponder and pray forward the future of the congregation. As we were discussing possibilities, one earnest person said, "Dr. Callahan, no one lives around us anymore. Everyone has moved to the suburbs."

Earlier I had walked the area around the church to see what I could see, as is my practice in all my consultations. In my walk the day before, I had seen several office buildings around the church, including a ten-story office highrise right across the street from the front door of the church.

Together we considered how many people worked in that building. It turned out that four of the people in our meeting that night worked there. They estimated that about 120 persons worked on each floor. There were more than 1,200 people who were *working* right across the street from that church.

Most worked in middle-management positions. Knowing that the average middle manager may spend seventy hours a week at work, I realized that where these persons *lived* was in the office building. They spent most of their waking hours there. Where they *slept* was in a bedroom community. That it is called a bedroom community is no accident.

The church actually had more persons *living* around it now than in an earlier time. What had fooled the congregation was that there were no longer any Victorian homes with green grass out front, children playing in the yards, and cars parked in the driveways. Now there were office buildings, and they were filled with persons who were *living* there most of their waking hours.

As we discussed it further, we examined several ways one could visit with individuals in that building. One of the simplest ways was to have breakfast with one of the church members in the building cafeteria. During the course of the breakfast, one would be likely to meet several other people from the office building, most of whom would not have a church home.

Another optimum time was lunch. Another was to visit over coffee after work for ten to fifteen minutes. Another was during a morning break; and yet another, during an afternoon break. The first three mentioned have little intrusion on the workplace. The fourth and fifth do somewhat.

I suggested the pastor phone and work out times to visit individually with each of his four members in the office building. He had lunch with one. He had breakfast with another. He visited with another during the morning break. The fourth member he visited during the afternoon break. In each case he arrived a few minutes early and met and visited with the several persons with whom each of his members worked. Over time he became the pastor for many of the people who work in that building.

As you consider the opportunities for work visits, I encourage you to use good judgment. You might visit with someone briefly during lunch—during the process you may

also meet some of the persons with whom they work and
live. You might discover some newcomers—people who
have been recently hired.

The best day to be in contact with persons where they
work is probably Thursday. The next best time is Wed-
nesday, followed by Tuesday. Those three days—with five
possibilities each—give you fifteen opportunities to contact
people personally without having to arrange an evening
when they are home and you are free to visit. Many people
are more easily found where they work than where they
sleep.

Table 5.1 indicates a possible schedule for work visiting.

Table 5.1 Work Visiting Possibilities

	Tuesday	Wednesday	Thursday
Breakfast			
Morning coffee			
Lunch			
Afternoon coffee			
After work			

Monday might not be the best day. In many instances
people are just organizing their workweek, and it can be a
fairly busy, confusing day. Friday might not be the best day
either. Many people have already left work on Friday. Their
bodies may still be there; their minds have already headed
elsewhere. You do have three excellent days in which to visit
persons in or near where they work.

It is natural to visit with people where they work. It is
how people visit with one another. In the process you will
come to know many more people in your community.

Both laity and pastors can do this. Phone a person you
would like to have the fun of visiting with—an occasional

worshiper, a constituent, a person served in mission, a relational unchurched person, a member. These persons all have direct, on-going linkages with your congregation. Suggest the possibility of visiting over lunch, breakfast, or a break time where they work.

This can be done on an occasional basis or on a more concentrated basis. For example, you can invest ten Thursdays during the course of a year visiting with people where they work. Mostly, you can visit with occasional worshipers, constituents, persons served in mission, and relational unchurched persons, as well as members.

Select ten Thursdays that are important in the life of the community and/or are prior to major Sundays in your congregation. On each of the Thursdays visit with five individuals. During each visit you may meet several people with whom that person works. By the end of your visiting, you may very well have met over one hundred people. Of these, approximately 70 percent will be unchurched. It would take countless evenings to accomplish the same range of community visitation. And this only describes what one person can accomplish in visiting with people where they work. When four persons do this, the sharing of compassion and the value to the community is multiplied in extraordinary ways.

Use your best wisdom and creativity. Many people don't work from 8 to 5, Monday through Friday. What I've shared above is suggestive, not exhaustive. You know best the work patterns in your community.

Focus on where you *can* visit. It's not always appropriate to visit with someone where they work. Sometimes a work visit is a follow-up visit. Sometimes a phone call is made to arrange such a visit. Keep your options flexible.

The biblical texts are clear. Jesus visited persons where they worked. He called some of the disciples from their work to his mission. Visiting with people where they work has been a long-standing pattern for Christians. Visiting has occurred in fields, near mills, on job sites, in markets, near coal mines, and many more places. Sometimes I think of our modern office buildings as the coal mine shafts of this time. Rather than digging deep into the earth, they rise high into the sky.

The work visit is one of the best ways to make contact with people. Many persons make thoughtful decisions over a breakfast or a lunch near where they work, and many are helped by sharing with a cheerful, compassionate person who has sought them out where they work.

PERSONAL PHONE CALLS

A phone call is one of the most effective means of visiting. Significant, helpful conversations occur over the phone. It is a popular means of demonstrating one's interest and caring. A personal phone call can be

- a visit with its own integrity
- for the purpose of working out a time to visit together

Both have value.

A personal phone call has its own integrity as a major form of visiting. It's not something we do because we think it may be easier than sharing a home or a work visit. It's not uncommon for people to make decisions about their lives during phone conversations. Feel free to take full advantage of this visiting possibility.

These recent technologies have strengthened visiting by phone:

- cellular and mobile phones
- video phones
- voice mail
- answering services
- answering machines

The personal cellular or mobile phone, which people increasingly carry with them in their cars or on their person, will make phone contacts even more natural and normal than they are now. Video phones, well used, will make future phone calls even more personal than they are now. Voice mail, answering services, and answering machines will continue to improve as means of being in touch with one another. The phone is already central in people's lives. It will become even more important as a primary form of communication with people.

In visiting by phone, we seek to help, not harass. Regrettably, people have experienced abuses and difficulties. We do not want to contribute to any of those. Respect a person's privacy and individual interests. Let our use of the phone represent the best in consideration, integrity, and good manners. Our mission is to share compassion and community. The personal phone call can do so in meaningful ways.

A personal phone call can also help us set up a time to visit. Some people ask me, "Dr. Callahan, do you think we should phone before we visit?" Sometimes it makes excellent sense to phone before you visit. You would certainly phone ahead to set up a time to visit with someone where they work—to have breakfast, lunch, or the like.

In some communities and with some persons, phoning ahead is a courtesy. Yet in other communities and with other persons, phoning before one visits would be considered an insult. You will know best the prevailing customs in your community.

The phone call can be the primary visit when that is your intent. I encourage you to be clear as to your purpose, whether it is a visit in itself or a preliminary conversation in order to arrange a time you can visit together at work, home, or in some community place.

When a personal phone visit is the helpful way forward, do it. When you really want to visit face-to-face, use the phone to schedule a time to get together.

Try not to switch purposes in midstream. Do not phone to discover a time to get together, then, finding that difficult, try to translate the phone call into the visit. Be clear about your purpose and stick with it.

PERSONAL NOTES

Receiving a personal note is like enjoying the sun coming up. It warms the day. A personal, handwritten message is one of the most effective ways of being in contact with people. In our time, people get few personal notes, although they get lots of mail.

You could write a simple three-sentence note. With first-time worshipers, a personal note mailed on Sunday or Monday might say,

Dear John and Mary,

Glad we could worship together this Sunday.
    As we can be helpful, we look forward to doing so.
    Feel free to phone. My number is 539-2443.

                                              Yours,
                                              Bill Freeman

A personal note written to relational persons might say,

Dear Jim and Sally,

I invite you to be part of our Christmas Eve service this coming Thursday at 7:30 P.M.

It will be a family time.
Come. Share. Be part of the family.

Yours,
Jean Cox

I am amazed at how many people tell me that personal notes had a decisive influence in their lives. A personal note is among the most thoughtful, considerate gestures we can share.

PERSONAL LETTERS

A personal letter is typed rather than handwritten and includes the person's name as an integral part of the letter. Word processors and computers can be used to produce good personal letters. The salutations—"Dear John and Mary"—don't look inserted. They are part and parcel of the letter. A photocopied or mimeographed letter with names inserted doesn't count as a personal letter. Regrettably, with some it is clear the name has been typed or written in. Some say "Dear first-time worshiper." These letters do more harm than good. They are institutional, organizational, functional.

By contrast, many people respond well to a short, sincere, warm personal note or letter.

Personal notes and personal letters can be delivered by

- postal service
- facsimile transmission (fax)
- various delivery services

The postal service will continue to be the primary way personal notes and letters are delivered. Still, people are increasingly communicating with one another by fax. As this practice becomes even more widespread, it will be natural to share notes and letters in this way. Some congregations are already doing so.

DECIDING WHAT TO CHOOSE

As you look at these five personal visiting possibilities, use your own good judgment to choose the ones that will work best for you in terms of

- the ways people visit with one another
- the community persons you seek to help
- your own gifts and competencies

I encourage you to look for the best ways forward. Don't get dragged down by worrying about which won't work in your community. By finding the best ways for you, you are not setting yourself up to fail. You are choosing constructive, successful ways forward.

6:

Visiting in Gatherings

People visit in gatherings, usually in

- small groups,
- large groups, or
- at community events.

Consider which of these best match your competencies and which you would have fun with.

In many communities, these gatherings provide opportunities to visit with

- occasional worshipers
- constituent families
- persons served in mission
- relational persons
- specific vocational groupings
- specific neighborhood groupings

Some communities and some congregations have gatherings to which newcomers are drawn, and these are prime opportunities for visiting with them.

We visit in gatherings to help people with their lives. We visit as a good friend, a good neighbor in Christ. Our visit has the spirit of

- How are things going?
- Any way we can help?

Our purpose is not to explain the church's program and activities. We are not trying to convince them to join. If you feel uncomfortable visiting in gatherings, you may be mistakenly assuming that your purpose is to promote church growth, and you see no easy way—particularly in community gatherings—to focus on that.

We would do well to follow the example of missionaries of old who mastered the art of circulating during gatherings. They did so

- as good friends and neighbors, with acts of kindness
- as good shepherds, caring for a specific human hurt and hope
- sharing Christ, as appropriate
- sometimes inviting persons to a community event of the congregation

They understood that their task was to be helpful—in simple ways—in people's lives. They were not there with tract and pamphlet. They were there with compassion and hope. We can do likewise in our time.

SMALL GROUP GATHERINGS

This is one of the best ways to visit with persons. Small groups usually gather in either the community or the church.

Sometimes you can best visit with persons in the small group gatherings that are natural, day-to-day occurrences in your community. Some groupings gather for breakfast or lunch. They gather at public meeting places:

- a restaurant
- a shopping area
- a truck stop
- a post office
- a library
- a bowling alley
- a country club

Consider the gatherings in your community. You don't need to organize anything. The group has already gathered itself. You can be a gentle, helpful presence in the group. You can share in the life of the group. Your witness will count.

Likewise you might gather a small group. You might organize it through a personal or work visit, a personal phone call, a personal note, or personal letter invitation. The gathering might take place in someone's home, at a public facility, or in your church building.

The persons who come will usually have something in common. Think through the glue that will help those attending discover one another. They may be recent newcomers, and this is a gathering of welcome. They may be preschool parents whose children are moving into kindergarten, and this is a resource gathering. They may have experienced the loss of a loved one. They may be wrestling with a specific human hurt or hope.

As people leave, you will hear them say, "You know, this was really helpful. It was fun. We should try this again."

The compassion and community that people discover in a small group gathering advance their pilgrimage toward God.

LARGE GROUP GATHERINGS

Like small group gatherings, large groups usually meet in either the community or the church.

Consider the large group gatherings that occur in your community. These gatherings may center around any of the following possibilities:

- family
- education
- vocation
- politics
- civic and community concerns
- recreation

PTA meetings are large group gatherings. Neighborhood clubs, professional associations, and sports and hobby clubs are frequently large group gatherings. Sometimes you visit with persons by being a helpful presence in these gatherings.

Likewise you can invite persons to be part of a large group gathering hosted by your congregation. Generally these have a spirit of celebration. People are invited by one or more of the other visiting contact methods. A principal opportunity to visit then occurs in the course of the gathering.

COMMUNITY EVENTS

Most communities have several major community events each year. These might be recreational events, civic gatherings, music concerts, or stage plays. They might be bazaars, flea markets, estate auctions, or community square-dancing events. In a sparsely populated area such as the outback of Australia, two of the best opportunities for visiting are during the sheep shearings and the cattle auctions. Think through those that have major significance in your community.

From one community to the next, there are distinctive events that capture the interest of people in that community. Even in large metropolitan areas, it is possible to discover the major community events to which persons are drawn. Feel free to use these occasions to visit with persons before, after, or during the events.

The first-century church had a particular genius for reaching out to persons in the midst of the community events of the empire. We can rediscover comparable possibilities in our time.

7 :

Special Ways of Visiting

People share and communicate in a wide range of ways, including some that are more indirect. This chapter focuses on six special ways of visiting with people that are less direct than a home visit or a phone call and that still do focus on the person. They are not mass media. The person does receive a specific contact. These six special possibilities that will help you communicate with persons are

- direct mail
- televisiting
- door invitations
- newsletters
- audio cassettes
- video cassettes

Consider which of these you might have fun doing, and match them with your strengths. Look also at which of these are the natural ways people are in communication with one another in your community. These special ways of visiting are likely to appeal to many people as they explore opportunities to reach out through visiting.

DIRECT MAIL

The best direct mail invitations match these criteria:

- They have a single focus and invite a single action.
- They show a spirit of compassion and a sense of community.
- They are simple and well designed.
- They are timely.

Direct mail can be to a geographical area, a life-stage grouping, a vocational grouping, or a specific human hurt and hope grouping.

The *single focus* may be the Christmas Eve service. People are invited to engage in a *single action*—to participate in the Christmas Eve service. The single focus, single action keeps the message simple. It doesn't overwhelm them with the details of everything going on during Advent.

Regrettably, we often do too much in a single piece of direct mail. We send multiple-focus, multiple-action pieces. We think we're saving money by making one mailing serve several purposes.

When people in the community receive a mailing with a busy, cluttered collection of events, they may feel that the only way they can be part of this congregation is to count on being very busy persons. That form of direct mail is relatively ineffectual.

The best direct mail keeps a single focus—simple and clear—whether on a Christmas Eve service, on a major community Sunday, or on an Easter service. Persons are invited to a single action—participating in that specific event.

You can create a series of invitations, sharing several direct-mail invitations with the same grouping over time. Thoughtful repetition helps; include these steps:

1. a single-focus, single-action invitation to your Christmas
    Eve service

2.   a single-focus, single-action invitation to a major com-
    munity Sunday in January or February

3. a multiple-focus, single-action invitation; lift up three
    events related to Easter; encourage them to participate
    in one

4. a multiple-focus, double-action invitation; highlight sev-
    eral events in your summer program; encourage them
    to participate in the two that interest them

    Then, you might consider another step:

5. a multiple-focus, multiple-action invitation to share in
    your congregation's fall program. Multiple focus, multi-
    ple action invitations have less value as an initial contact.
    Their value increases once you have sent the first four in-
    vitations.

Because people are drawn to the Christian movement
primarily by demonstrations of *compassion* and *community,* direct-mail invitations that live out those values will be
particularly effective. Especially on a mission field, you will
have less success using direct-mail pieces that challenge people, ask them to deepen their commitment, and suggest a
sense of responsibility. These motivations do not resonate
with most persons in the community you are trying to reach.

The motivational invitations that share a message of
compassion and community—expressed in colors, textures,
print style, pictures, words, and text—are most helpful. I
commend to you the discussion on motivation that can be
found in my book *Effective Church Finances.*

The best direct-mail invitations are *simple* and *well designed.* They appeal to the grouping you seek to invite. When

you are sending an invitation to families with children, for example, consider a design, spirit, and message that they can relate to. If you're mailing an invitation to a blue-collar community, a piece that is elaborate, fancy, and opulent would communicate less well. Its message would be read, "If you're not part of the wealthy upper class, you don't belong."

Direct mail is most effective when it is also *timely*. This may surprise you, but the fact is, many people go to a Christmas Eve service or a major community Sunday on impulse, not after planning. If your invitation arrives three weeks in advance, it will be less effective. It will get lost in the shuffle. Plan instead to have your invitation arrive within one to three days in advance of the event. That's when many people will say, "Oh, this looks really interesting. Let's go." The most timely invitation to a Christmas Eve service, therefore, arrives within three days of Christmas Eve.

Yes, there is considerable power in direct-mail invitations when they are well done.

TELEVISITING

Televisiting can be used

- to conduct research
- to issue an invitation
- to share information
- to leave a brief message

When you use the phone for *research*, you are calling to secure brief, concise information from those being contacted. For example, you might ask them to share two major community interests or concerns. Many people are pleased to know that a church is interested in the needs and concerns of the community. The focus is on discovering information helpful to the church's mission. It is a succinct survey or research project.

You may wish to use televisiting in order to *invite* people to a major community Sunday or a special event. This form of televisiting usually occurs in the week preceding the event.

Another use of televisiting is *to inform*. In seeking to share information, the callers ask about the possibility of sending resources

- for a specific human hurt or hope
- about a concern in the community
- about a new congregation being formed
- about a special event your congregation is sharing

A reasonable number of those called usually say, "Yes, send me something." The more positive responses are shaped by the quality and value of the event, the care with which the group being called has been selected, the spirit and voice of the caller, and the time of day.

You may also wish to use televisiting to leave a *message*. A telecomputer system dials numbers from a specific selection or at random. It sends a short, helpful message—from ten to twenty seconds. People may be given the opportunity to respond by leaving a message on the telecomputer's answering system.

All four forms of televisiting are helpful. Over several years you might take advantage of the benefits of each. Feel free to do them in whatever sequence suits the persons you hope to reach.

DOOR INVITATIONS

Another special possibility is a door invitation. In an area of homes, shops, or offices, simply place on each door an invitation to a major community Sunday or a special event. People discover the invitation and look at it quickly. When it meets the criteria already discussed in the section on direct mail, that door invitation will be effective.

Sometimes the door invitations are put on the windshields of cars in a nearby shopping center parking lot. If you are seeking to reach a specific vocational grouping, you might place the invitations on the windshields of cars parked near where people in this grouping work.

Yes, there are places where this is not allowed. And, yes, there are many places where this is effectively done and has a positive effect. Ensure a minimum of negative impact by thoughtful distribution. You don't want your efforts remembered only as papers blowing down the street. Do it well.

NEWSLETTERS

Most communities have a range of circulating newsletters. Feel free to be in direct contact with persons through one or more of these newsletters:

• life stage
• vocational
• civic and community

For example, in many communities there are newsletters circulated among

• parents with preschool children
• parents with elementary school children
• early-retired persons

Share an invitation, an article, or an interview in any one of these life-stage newsletters.

Do likewise with vocational newsletters, whether they are for workers in a textile mill, teachers, construction workers, lawyers, doctors, hotel service personnel, stock-brokers, farmers—the list could go on.

The newsletters aimed at civic and community group-ings in your area are also worth considering. Sometimes these newsletters focus on specific hobbies or interests. Place an ad or a news release there from time to time.

You could create your own newsletter—something short-term that would be helpful in people's lives. Perhaps, for example, your community is experiencing rapid growth and has many newcomers, particularly during the sum-mer—June through September. A short-term, one-summer newsletter can welcome them. You could publish one issue for the whole summer or four issues—one for each month, June through September.

The newsletter can help them with their search for roots, place, and belonging, for family and community. Don't make it solely a church-focused newsletter. Let the focus be on their lives. Newcomers appreciate the welcom-ing newsletter that helps them to be part of the community.

You might also consider doing a cooperative newslet-ter with a community grouping. Your church may have a mission with a specific human hurt or hope, and a commu-nity grouping may also be seeking to be helpful with the same human hurt or hope.

You might get together on a short-term, seasonal news-letter that provides resources for that specific need. Explore the possibilities. You may discover many community group-ings that are open to working with you.

AUDIO AND VIDEO CASSETTES

You can develop audio and/or video tapes to share with peo-ple. For example, you can create a recorded message to help first-time worshipers. On the cassette, share some of the fol-lowing:

- specific mission possibilities where their lives can count
- the future toward which your congregation is headed
- the ways they can benefit from and participate in the shepherding of your congregation
- the possibilities available for their personal growth and development in the Christian life
- the groupings through which they can discover roots, place, belonging, a sense of community

In such a recorded message, spend your time on the future, not the past. New people can't participate in the past. They can share in the future. Share a people-centered spirit. Spend little time describing your facilities.

For newcomers, a comparable recording can help orient them to the centers of life in your community. Consider similar cassettes for other groupings. The cassettes can be dropped off where people live or work, or they can be mailed or distributed at small group or large group gatherings. They can be available during community events. The same criteria we discussed for direct mail apply here. The quality of the recording needs to be excellent. When it shares well the message of compassion and hope, people respond.

I have spoken constructively of all of the possible ways of visiting—five personal, three gathering, six special—fourteen in all. Several of these will be helpful in your mission.

What takes wisdom is determining which of the ways will work well for you. Fortunately, you have many possibilities. Choose well. God will bless your mission.

Community Persons	Home Visits	Work Visits	Personal Phone Calls	Personal Notes	Personal Letters	Small Group Gatherings	Large Group Gatherings	Community Events	Direct Mail	Televisiting	Door Invitations	Newsletters	Audiocassettes	Videocassettes
First-time Worshipers														
Newcomers														
Occasional Worshipers														
Constituent Families														
Persons Served in Mission														
Relational Persons														
Specific Vocational Groupings														
Specific Neighborhood Groupings														
Inactives														

Instructions: Choose the one to three ways of visiting that will be most helpful with the persons you have selected to visit. Mark these on the chart.

STEP THREE :

The Best Timing

8:

A Simple Approach

THE BEST TIMING

Decisive visits change our lives and shape our destinies. Many of us are who we have become because someone sought us out at a crucial time in our lives. Their visit was timely and helpful.

The best timing enhances the effectiveness of our visits. Just one visit with the best timing can help a person to grow.

Discover the persons you feel led to visit in year one. Choose your ways of visiting. Then, with wisdom and prayer, consider when the best time would be.

To be sure, any time is a good time. A visit anytime is better than no visit at all. When you are visiting, you are sharing an extraordinary gift with the person you visit, and that person will grace your life as well.

Yet the best timing saves your time. One visit at the best time is worth three to five visits at any other time. You want to visit with persons when their anticipation and anxiety levels are at their highest, when their search for compassion and community are the most profound. Then they are open and ready to advance their lives and their futures.

Each of the community groupings has a best time. The following suggestions are based on research and experience with many congregations. Use these suggestions as guidelines. They're not intended as absolute laws set in stone. They will provide you with clues and handles as you develop your visiting outreach. Feel free to improve on these suggestions in ways that suit your community.

FIRST-TIME WORSHIPERS

The best timing is

- on Sunday morning
- by Monday evening

You can share the first visit with first-time worshipers on Sunday morning. You need not wait until later in the week. In many congregations, certain persons are asked to serve as *new person greeters.*

New person greeters are distinct from door greeters. Door greeters stand at the entrance to the church and welcome each person. New person greeters stand away from the door. As best they can, they know those who come regularly well enough to recognize those who are new. And they know how to look for the person who appears puzzled, somewhat uncertain as to where to go. Often these are signs of a first-time worshiper.

The new person greeter moves to the new person, offering a word of welcome in a warm, winsome way. He or she usually engages the new person in a brief conversation. New person greeters don't hassle or hustle the first-time worshiper. They don't give a great deal of church program information.

This first, brief visit is personal and relational, not institutional and organizational. It is not information seeking or information giving. The focus is a simple, welcoming visit.

Again and again, in thousands of interviews, I have asked people why they decided to make a particular congregation their church home. Over and over, they say, "The first Sunday we came, Mary so warmly welcomed us, we just knew we had found our church home."

The names vary; the spirit remains the same. Consistently they were welcomed by a person who helped them feel at home.

You can never make the first impression a second time. Often the first impression is this visit with a new person greeter in the few minutes before the service. It doesn't take large groups of people welcoming first-time worshipers. That can be overwhelming and intimidating. It takes this one person who helps the first-time worshiper feel at home.

Eighty percent of people's decisions about choosing a new church home are based on what does or does not happen on a Sunday morning, and by Monday evening. Don't trust studies that say people attend many times before they make up their minds about a church. Those studies were done only among the people who came back! None of those studies interviewed the people who did not come back, who attended only once.

Thus, the best time to be in visiting contact with first-time worshipers is Sunday morning and by Monday evening. The contact by Monday evening could be

- a home visit—brief, informal, and welcoming
- a personal phone call—relational and simple
- a personal note—thoughtful and helpful, mailed Sunday afternoon or Monday morning
- a personal letter—positive and confirming, mailed Sunday afternoon or Monday morning

Share some form of a personal follow-up by Monday evening.

Waiting until Thursday has a diminished return. The effect of the best timing will have worn off. Or we may fail to follow up at all—maybe because we think they are simply shopping around for a church home. Much more is happening in the lives of first-time worshipers than that.

The decisive best timing is to share the third contact by Monday evening. Yes, the *third* contact. In their eyes, the first visit occurred when they came to worship with us on Sunday morning. The second visit happened between them and our new person greeter. When we make a follow-up visit, we're sharing the third visit. It's the neighborly, reciprocal kind of visit shared between people seeking to be good friends. It's a helping visit.

NEWCOMERS

The best timing includes

- during the four months of the highest density move-in to your community
- within three to five weeks of a family's moving in

Be aware of your community's patterns and statistics regarding when people move out and move in. In some southern retirement areas, most of the activity takes place from January through April. Many retirees enjoy their last northern Christmas with family in December, then move south during the first four months of the year. In many communities, most move-ins occur from May through August. With others, it is June through September. Visit with newcomers during the four months of highest move-in activity. Year-round visiting, although it is certainly possible, is not necessary. If you cannot do so throughout the year, at least do so during the four months of the most move-in activity.

Once you find out the four months that work best in your community, contact newcomers within the first three to five weeks of their move. Welcome them as part of the community.

Some newcomers will have participated regularly in their previous church homes. During their first few weeks in a new community, even formerly active churchgoers decide whether or not to participate in a new church. They either decide to continue the habit or they begin to get out of the habit.

Persons who were not previously active in church will be most open to beginning new behavior patterns after moving. Many people use the occasion of a move to start new lives. They hope life will be better for them in their new home. They have a sense of anticipation—and anxiety. If you wait until they've been there three or four months, you'll miss that window of opportunity. One visiting contact during those first few weeks is worth four visits at some later point.

OCCASIONAL WORSHIPERS

The best timing is during the week prior to a major community Sunday, especially those that suit

- specific human hurts and hopes
- life stages and life thresholds
- community concerns and interests

Share constructive resources on that major community Sunday that will provide occasional worshipers with handles of help and hope.

Share another contact with them prior to your next major community Sunday. In this way you increasingly have the opportunity to be a resource in their lives. Their relationship with God and the strength of their lives will advance.

Focus on your congregation's ten major community Sundays during the year. You may find it particularly helpful to share a visit sometime during February, March, or April. Many persons discover Christ as we head into Easter.

Remember, occasional worshipers are those who worship with us on Christmas and/or Easter and now and then at other times during the year. Their message to us is that they're in a "dating" stage. In romantic relationships, people go out on a first date, then they date again. They decide to go steady. They become engaged; then they get married. Likewise people discover church resources for their lives in gradual stages. Occasional worshipers are teaching us that this is their church home. Otherwise they would occasionally worship with some other congregation. They have almost claimed our congregation as their church family.

CONSTITUENT FAMILIES

The best timing is September through December. In many congregations, the programs and activities start afresh during this time. Thus an excellent time to contact these persons is as the strength and vitality of these programs is felt in strong, new ways.

Constituent families are not members; someone in the family participates in one of your church's groupings or activities. They know something about your church. They may or may not be Christians. By visiting with them, you may help them toward their Christian journey.

The best timing is during the four months when your programs begin in new ways—whatever months of the year that may be. In Australia programs start anew from

February through May, following the southern hemisphere summer. We would contact persons during these months.

When your congregation has a preschool, the enrollment period is the best timing. Visit with the constituent preschool family during the two to four weeks following their child's enrollment. In their eyes, they have become a constituent family in the church's preschool from the time they enroll. Welcome them as part of the church family. When the enrollment is in January through March, don't wait until September. Get on board with them at the same time they get on board with you.

This same principle applies to many of the activities in your congregation. Be in contact with persons when your groupings and activities are at their best.

PERSONS SERVED IN MISSION

The best timing is the week of a celebrative event or an anniversary event. This is when people are helped in fresh, new ways.

Your pastor may have performed a wedding with a couple that is living in the community. As they begin the second year of their marriage, your visit will help greatly.

A child may have been baptized. Share a visit a year later during the week of the child's birth or baptism. Focus on the health and well-being of the whole family.

There may have been a visit at the time of a major surgery. People remember a year later the trauma, the difficulty, and the help-giving resources shared during that time. A good time to visit them is during the week of the anniversary. People are very open to Christ on the anniversary of such an event in their lives.

It may be that your pastor has conducted a funeral for a family in the community. Share the visit during the week of the anniversary—particularly the first anniversary of the death of their loved one. Your visit will help with the grieving, and with new life.

RELATIONAL PERSONS

The best timing is October, November, and December as we head toward Christmas. People experience feelings of loneliness, isolation, and separation from family more during this time of the year than at any other time. The high number of suicides near Christmas is no mere coincidence.

It is a time when many persons are reminded that their own extended family is scattered across the land. They may have fledgling friends here, or perhaps a distant relative, yet they will not be with their primary family at Christmas.

Lots of people find Christ at Christmas. This is particularly true of relational community persons who already have some connection with someone in your congregation. Share a generous visit with them during October through December.

SPECIFIC VOCATIONAL GROUPINGS

The best timing relates to the life patterns of the specific vocational grouping you seek to visit. All vocational groupings have a rhythm of life across the year. For farmers, it revolves around the harvest. For construction workers, the peak is the summer season. For salespersons, it relates to the key seasons for sales of their products. Put yourself in their place. Look at their lives through their eyes. Discover the specific celebrative events in their own vocational patterns of life across the year. As best you can, visit them during the week of those celebrative events. This is usually the best timing.

A second-best timing would be the week prior to a major community Sunday. This is particularly true for those

Sundays that seek to offer resources to those in specific vocations. For example, you may have decided that one major community Sunday will focus on teachers in your community. Schedule it during a best time of year in relation to the rhythm of their own vocation. June, July, and August may not be optimal in the Northern Hemisphere. You will need to assess whether the best timing in your community is the beginning of school, the beginning of the second semester, or near the end of the school year.

SPECIFIC NEIGHBORHOOD GROUPINGS

The best timing is during the week prior to a major community Sunday. Invite all those who live in that specific neighborhood to be part of the service of worship on that Sunday. As best you can, develop that major community Sunday's focus on a specific human hurt and hope, a life stage, or an interest that is particularly important to that neighborhood. People will respond to the thoughtfulness of your contact prior to such an event.

INACTIVES

The best time to visit those church members who are inactive is during the week of a celebrative event such as a birthday, or during the anniversary week of a shepherding event such as the death of a loved one. The focus of the visit in both instances is sharing and caring with the person.

The best timing saves time. I have shared the basics of the principle so you can use your own wisdom and compassion. When you visit at the best possible time for each individual, you will be more effective in reaching people for God's mission.

9 :

Life Stages and Celebrative Events

THE POWER OF THE MOMENT

God reaches out to people in the moment. We are who we are because God reached out to us at a decisive time. God gives us moments of the best timing.

Because there is power in the moment, we will do well to time our visits to take advantage of certain important events and distinct stages in people's lives.

Consider these five best times as they relate to your community and your decisions about whom to visit:

- life stages
- celebrative events
- anniversary events
- significant seasons
- major community Sundays

LIFE STAGES

In this life's pilgrimage, we all live forward, passing through a series of life stages. With each new one we discover a new set of issues and possibilities we had not seen before and are not likely to see again. Each threshold presents occasions and opportunities for growth and development.

People experience strong anticipation and towering anxiety as they approach new life stages. These are decisive occasions. People are extraordinarily open to their own growth and improvement.

All people may not necessarily experience all of these life stages. Some people never retire. Some persons, with honor and integrity, decide not to marry and indeed live rich, full lives as single persons. Families can include single-person families, single-parent, double-parent, blended, separated, and divorced families. In our time people share in one or more of these family groupings throughout their lives. The following life thresholds are stages, not ages.

Early marriage. Some persons are "early marrieds" in their fifties; some are in their late thirties. It is a stage, not an age.

Preschool families. In our time this is one of the toughest life thresholds into which families enter.

Early elementary. Usually grades one through three.

Late elementary. Usually grades four through six. Sometimes grades four and five, when the pattern is a middle school.

Junior high. Sometimes this is middle school. It is a significant, frequently difficult life threshold that affects both the students and their families. It is important to note that the anticipation and anxiety levels are at their highest in the spring prior to entering junior high. The best time to help families in this stage is in the spring. The students' minds, concerns, interests, and anxieties, as well as those of their families, get to junior high in the spring; their bodies get there in the fall.

High school. Likewise teenagers and their families move into this life stage in the spring of the last year in junior high or middle school. Spring, therefore, is the best time to offer help. That is when people are most open to resources that will help them with their anticipation and anxiety levels.

College. Some people head to college, and some, beyond that, to graduate school.

Work. Some head directly to work from high school or without finishing junior high or high school.

Single/professional. Many persons focus their energies on their vocations. With integrity they decide to be single. Single persons are whole persons, with competent vocations, making constructive contributions in the community.

Midlife development. An earlier term for this stage was *midlife crisis.* It is more of a stage than an age. It appears to happen when people sense that they are at the halfway point in their life's pilgrimage.

Open horizons. The earlier term was *empty nest.* I don't know for sure, but I imagine that the earlier term was developed by a young sociologist whose children were small. He or she looked years ahead to the time their children would be grown and gone and grieved over their leaving.

Most of the people with whom I visit whose children are grown and gone, by contrast, talk about all the things they can do now that they couldn't do before. It is a time of open horizons! And their biggest fear is that the children might move back.

Pre-retirement. Generally this is the three- to five-year period before a person plans to retire. Keep in mind that some people retire more than once in their lifetime.

After people retire, they experience virtually as many life stages from early retirement to older adult as there are from ages one to thirty, or thirty to sixty. It is not appropriate to lump all retired persons together in one life stage. There are yet many life stages through which persons pass following retirement. These include

- Early retirement
- Retirement
- Late retirement
- Early older adult
- Older adult

Each of these stages may be from three to five years in length.

Remember, these are life stages, not ages. In one congregation I met a woman in her late eighties who described her sense of satisfaction and joy as she helped "older adults." As we talked further, I learned that most of the older persons she was helping were in their early seventies. They had already promoted themselves right past her to the life stage of "older adult."

Among the best times to visit with persons is as they are moving toward one of these significant life thresholds. People make solid decisions for their futures as they approach a new life stage.

CELEBRATIVE EVENTS

Share some form of visit with persons during the week of a celebrative event in their lives or the life of their family. These events include birthdays, anniversaries, significant family good times, graduations, weddings, reunions. Celebrative events include promotions at work, new discoveries about one's strengths, gifts, competencies, and so on. People are extraordinarily open to a caring visit at high points in their lives, at times of joy.

ANNIVERSARY EVENTS

Share some visiting contact with persons during the week of a significant anniversary. By this I mean a *shepherding* anniversary, not a wedding anniversary. I have more in mind the anniversary of an illness or surgery from which they have significantly recovered.

For some persons, the anniversary of a tragic accident is a time when they reexperience its trauma. You can reach out to them in shepherding ways. You can reach out to people on the anniversary of the loss of their spouse or some other family member or a close friend.

SIGNIFICANT SEASONS

Share a visit with persons in the name of Christ during an important season of the year. Those who have yet to discover Christ are not likely to be familiar with the Christian seasons of Advent or Lent. Those are "inside the church" terms.

Even so, it is clear that one of the best times of the year to be in contact with people is during the Christmas season—the month from Thanksgiving to Christmas. Many persons think of that as a major shopping season—and it is, in our culture. Many people in retail consider it the principal business season of the year. It's a time of anticipation and business and busyness. As a significant season in our culture, it's among the best times to be in contact with persons.

A second significant season for visiting is the spring. Something about the reawakening of dormant life in spring helps us sense another opportunity for self-renewal. Visits during this season touch the heartstrings of hope perhaps more than at any other season.

MAJOR COMMUNITY SUNDAYS

I encourage congregations to have—in addition to Christmas and Easter—up to eight major community Sundays a year. A major community Sunday may focus on

- a life stage
- a specific human hurt and hope
- a community concern and interest
- a major mission grouping

Many mission congregations have eight major community Sundays a year during which they share resources of help with community persons.

A "church Sunday" is something like Pentecost. It's a significant event for those inside the faith, but it doesn't have relevance for people in the community. Feel free to have forty-two church Sundays a year, then share ten major community Sundays, including Easter and Christmas. It will be like having Christmas ten times a year. One of the best times to visit with persons is the week prior to a major community Sunday.

You may discover other best times. I encourage you to do so. If you keep in mind the five best times discussed in this chapter, you will have a streamlined, focused approach. God will richly bless your visiting outreach.

VISITING, NOT ORGANIZING

God calls us to visit, not to organize. Invest your time in visiting people, not in organizing files. Have a preference for slightly unorganized visiting over a fully organized file system. Develop a "fast break" approach to visiting. Don't spend great amounts of time setting up a neat, tidy file system.

Keep your focus on people and their lives. Have just enough organization so you can begin visiting. The best way to do visiting is to begin visiting.

Some person—volunteer or staff—will help organize a file system as your visiting grows. When they do, call it the community visiting file, not the prospect file. We are visiting, not prospecting. The focus is on the mission.

You don't need a complete file system before the first visit occurs. Had that been the case in the first century, the mission of the early church would have been in considerable jeopardy.

That old friend, a compulsion for perfection, can stifle the enthusiasm with which you begin. Perfectionism tells us that nothing should fall through the cracks. Compulsiveness about organizing full file systems for visiting drains considerable time, energy, and creativity—and gets in the way of visiting. Meister Eckhart, a medieval Christian mystic, once wrote, "The devil has a device called 'busyness' by which he deceives Christians into thinking they are doing the will of God."

Some people spend so much time on the busyness of organizing the files that they hardly ever visit. Be at peace. In the early stages of your visiting, have a preference for slightly uncoordinated visiting. Your outreach will grow. Start by simply visiting. Keep first things first. A file system can't visit. You can.

Once you've started visiting, you will know better what you want to keep a file on. Match your file to your visiting. Don't build your visiting based on the file system. Visit. Your file system will grow sufficient unto the needs of your visiting. Develop a simple approach. Take seriously the *best timing* for visiting, and begin.

Community Persons

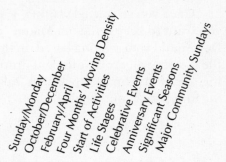

Community Persons	Sunday/Monday	October/December	February/April	Four Months' Moving Density	Start of Activities	Life Stages	Celebrative Events	Anniversary Events	Significant Seasons	Major Community Sundays
First-time Worshipers										
Newcomers										
Occasional Worshipers										
Constituent Families										
Persons Served in Mission										
Relational Persons										
Specific Vocational Groupings										
Specific Neighborhood Groupings										
Inactives										

Instructions: Choose the best timing for the persons you plan to visit. Mark these on the chart.

STEP FOUR:

Your Gifts for Visiting

10:

Gifts and Graces

SPECIFIC GIFTS

We can claim and nurture our gifts and graces for visiting. Over the years, I have observed that those who visit best are persons who

- have fun in visiting
- share friendships easily and naturally
- have longings to help with specific human hurts and hopes
- possess a confident hope and vision for the future
- have a deep and abiding compassion for God's mission

Consider these specific competencies. Grow them in yourself. Look for a visiting partner who is growing these qualities in her or his own life.

When you visit, have fun. Avoid the twins of doom and gloom. Leave behind any tendency to whine and complain, lament and bemoan. It is a gift to be able to have genuine fun seeking out persons in the name of God. Grow the gift. Develop a sense of grace and peace. Relax, have fun, enjoy life, live in Christ. Once you do, you'll be able to enrich the lives of others through your visits.

A SENSE OF CARING

I encourage you to share distinctive gifts with the distinctive persons you visit. Meet their needs. For example, share these specific gifts and graces with

- first-time worshipers: a sense of caring
- newcomers: a sense of welcoming
- occasional worshipers: a sense of inviting
- relational persons: a sense of belonging

Each of these gifts corresponds to the specific human hurts and hopes of these persons. In a spirit of prayer, consider the simple ways you can share these gifts and be open to discovering others.

With *first-time worshipers,* the best gift is a sense of caring. For most first-time worshipers, some precipitating event in their lives has stirred their longings for God and church. Can we also share a sense of welcoming, inviting, and belonging? Yes, and most especially share a sense of caring.

In our culture, going to church is no longer the thing to do. Nowadays most people aren't shopping around for a church home. Some precipitating event has occurred. Don't expect them to tell you about what has happened that has led them to church. Simply know that something is going on in their lives. Would you or I candidly tell people we've just met that the reason we're here this morning is that our marriage is virtually falling apart? No. We'd say—with a smile on our face—"Thank you very much. We're just looking around for a church home."

Would you or I say, "Well, the reason we're here this morning is that we have a fourteen-year-old. We don't know what to do with him, and he doesn't know what to do with us." No. We'd say—with a smile on our face—"Thank-you very much. We're just looking around for a church home."

Would you or I say, "The reason we're here this morning is that one of our best friends was just killed in a tragic auto accident, and we are reminded of how precious and precarious life really is."

Would you or I say, "The reason we're here this morning is that we've just learned that a family member has a terminal illness." No. We'd probably say—with a smile on our face—"Thank-you very much. We're just looking around for a church home."

So when first-time worshipers tell you that they're just looking around for a church, you can know there is probably more to it than that. Something more is happening in their lives than they are ready to talk about. Even church people who have moved to a new community and come to a church on Sunday morning may say, "Well, we're just looking around for a church," when the real reason they're there is that the move has been more difficult than they had anticipated.

Your visit—with a special sense of caring—will be most helpful. First-time worshipers may never tell you what is hurting deep inside them. That's fine. The gift you share is caring. Many people are helped through a troubled time by someone who shares a sense of caring.

The focus of your visit is *relational,* not functional. Help it to be a person-centered visit. This visit is not a time to dwell on the organization of your church. Focus on the person you are visiting.

The following suggestions will help. They also apply to your follow-up visit, phone call, or note. Avoid saying something like this:

> "Those of you who are visiting with us this morning, we want you to know how glad we are that you are visiting with us, and we hope you will come back and visit with us when you can."

Three things in that statement are not helpful. First, look how many times "you" and "us" are said. They came hoping that there would not be too many barriers. Every time you say "you" and "us" or "you" and "we" you raise another barrier.

Second, the statement suggests they are "visiting." They are not simply visiting. They came to worship, not to visit. Something is happening in their lives. We trivialize it by referring to their coming as a "visit."

The third problem is with the phrase "we hope you will come back and visit with us when you can." By saying this, we confirm that we do not understand that something is happening in their lives. We teach them that we think this is simply a functional, institutional exercise in shopping-around-for-a-church.

Instead, consider this possibility. You could say,

> "Those of you who are worshiping for the first time, *Welcome*. We are glad we can worship God together this morning. As we can be helpful, we look forward to doing so."

The spirit of the statement shares a sense of caring. There are no "you" and "us" barriers. We are worshiping *together*. The first-time worshiper is *in* from the first Sunday. The phrase "as we can be helpful" is more shepherding. "*If* we can be helpful" would be too conditional and would sound as though we would help only in an emergency. The phrase "we look forward to doing so" is more intentional. The phrase "feel free to contact us" would be too organizational. With the first-time worshiper, share a sense of caring.

A SENSE OF WELCOMING

With *newcomers*, the best gift is a sense of welcoming. I encourage you to draw on your welcoming skills when visiting with persons who have just moved to the community. The experience of moving probably wasn't all it was cut out to be. The new job hasn't turned out to be exactly what had been promised. The new house isn't quite as comfortable as the last one. The children play in the yard all summer long, and yet the neighborhood kids still don't accept them. Moving is tough.

In sharing an immediate sense of welcoming, you could say,

> "Welcome. I have come to welcome you as part of the community. We're glad you're in the community."

The message is clear. The newcomers are welcomed into the community as they move in. Yes, we can also share a sense of caring, inviting, and belonging. Most especially, share a sense of welcoming.

It doesn't help to think of the newcomer as a stranger. Avoid saying something like,

> "I understand you are new in the neighborhood. I thought I would drop by and welcome you to our community."

The first sentence shares something they already know, and they know that we know. Many newcomers are slightly self-conscious about being new. Why say something we both already know and, further, that runs the risk of making them yet more self-conscious?

The phrase "I thought I would drop by" implies you were really headed somewhere else. It tells them this visit is an interruption for you. This is really a throwaway. This is incidental. It doesn't really count.

The phrase "welcome you to our community" teaches them that they are still outsiders. It is *our* community. It is not yet their community. The message is that we have not yet taken a vote to include them. We will take that vote after they have been here a while. It is still *our* community.

Many newcomers have looked forward to a new start. This is a major reason people move. We can help them with their new start. We don't have to ask lots of questions. We don't need to wonder about their past. We can welcome them to a new life and include them for who they are now.

A SENSE OF INVITING

With *occasional worshipers*, the best gift is a sense of inviting. These are people who have already claimed your congregation as their church home. By their occasional presence they are indicating that if they had a church home, it would be your congregation.

Sometimes it helps to intentionally invite them more fully into the fellowship of the congregation. An easy, natural way to do this may be to invite them to be part of a one-time event or a short-term fellowship, recreation, or study group. The invitation might be to share in a mission team project, a work project, or a retreat. Your invitation is to some event where they can deepen their relationship within your congregation. Each person grows at his or her own pace. It does no good to push. It is helpful to invite.

A SENSE OF BELONGING

With *relational persons*, the best gift is a sense of belonging. It is like a spirit of family. Avoid distractions that lead to talking about committees, membership, church organization, or the institution. Relational persons already have an acquaintance, work association, friendship, or family relationship with someone in the congregation. What they look for is a sense of belonging, of family, of being included.

The best time to reach out to relational persons is as Christmas approaches. Here is a sample of what you might say in a visit with them:

"We'd like you to be part of our congregational family
this Christmas. We invite you to share in our family
Christmas Eve service."

Here are some things to avoid saying:

"I know that you know so-and-so in our church,
and so I came by to invite you to attend church this
coming Sunday."
   "You know, there is a membership orientation
class—no obligation—two Sundays from now. You
might want to just sit in on that. You won't have to
sign on the dotted line."

Keep the focus on the congregation as family. Steer
clear of talking about institutional and organizational mat-
ters. Relational persons look for roots, place, and belonging.
Share the gift of a sense of belonging.

11:

Training and Praying

STEPS

God invites us to visit. Invest most of your energy in visiting and only some in training. The purpose is to visit, not to train. Some people spend so much time in training that they hardly visit.

The longer the training program, the higher the drop-out rate. And, worse, the longer the training program, the less visiting you do, and the fewer the people who will be visited on behalf of God's mission.

Consider two factors. You have

- reasonable competencies for visiting
- the capacity to develop your strengths for visiting

Devise a simple training program. These self-development steps will help you grow:

- visit several good matches
- discuss with other visitors
- study visiting resources
- share in a coaching conference

- visit, visit, visit
- pray
- visit people you hope will be visitors

GOOD MATCHES

Visit first with several good matches. Select some persons, some families, who are a good match for you. The match may be common life stages, relational, vocational, or a mutual interest. You will get on well during your early visits. This will help you grow your sense of confidence and competence.

DISCUSSIONS

Initiate the opportunity to discuss your visiting experiences with others who visit. Do this from time to time during the year. Don't turn this into a weekly or monthly routine.

I encourage you to select a team partner, primarily for the purpose of sharing resources and learning with each other. Have the fun of breakfast or lunch together. Talk over common experiences in visiting. Make it an occasional, intentional time.

RESOURCES

Study and share visiting resources. As others begin visiting, provide each with a copy of this book. Encourage them to study it well and to find a team partner with whom they can discuss the book. When you find other resources that are helpful, share them.

Let this book do much of your training. Given half a chance, people have a genuine capacity for creativity, ingenuity, discovery, and self-development.

COACHING CONFERENCE

Once a year hold an informal coaching conference for those who are visiting in the community. Include a time for

- celebration, good fun, and good times
- study of this book
- coaching and sharing with one another
- prayer and support

Let the coaching conference be good fun, brief, and helpful. Build a sense of community. Gather for two to four hours, not too long. Share what you've learned about visiting. Take advantage of the benefits of this book; study some part of it each time. Discuss it, internalize it, act on it. Share new insights that have come to you as you have been visiting. Coach one another. Pray together. As new visitors come on board, include them in this annual coaching conference.

VISIT

We learn from experience. We learn visiting as we visit. The three keys are visit, visit, visit. We discover new insights and grow personally as we visit frequently. This doesn't have to be year-round. It can be for a short time—three to four months. Visiting is best learned firsthand.

PRAY

Pray. Pray. Pray. It will help develop your competencies for visiting. Pray as you study this book. Let your discussions and coaching conferences with your team partner be rich experiences of prayer.

Pray before you visit. Pray before you write the personal note. Pray before you make the personal phone call. Pray before you knock on the door.

Pray for the person you are visiting. Have the sense that you are sent of God to visit with this person. Pray not so much for yourself, that you will do well. Focus your prayers on the person you are visiting. As you pray, think of your best friends, and pray that you will discover some new best friends. You will be amazed at how many new best friends respond to your note, answer the phone, and open the door.

Pray that you will sense the presence of God in your visit. Know that God is with you as you visit. Your visit will become an expression of God's grace.

NEW VISITORS

As you visit, you learn visiting. As you visit, others learn visiting from you. Visiting is something not so much taught as learned. People learn visiting from the example of visiting you share when you visit them.

People visit in direct relation to the ways they have experienced being visited. The best way to help people learn visiting is to visit them. New visitors usually come from among the people who have been visited, and some of those you visit will eventually become visitors themselves. Your visits have been helpful in their lives, and they want to share the same joy and compassion.

Indeed, consider visiting with persons you hope will become visitors. Should you sense that a person has gifts and competencies for visiting, the best thing you can do is to visit them. The focus of the visit is on them, however, not on recruiting them for the church's visiting program.

Have in mind several persons whom you might invite a year from now to be part of a visiting team. Visit them during the coming year. As you do so, you'll be growing your own visiting competencies and demonstrating the value of person-to-person visits, so that when you do invite them to visit, they'll be more likely to accept.

GROW YOURSELF FORWARD

I have discovered these simple, straightforward steps in my own visiting. I'm certain they will benefit you as you grow and develop your own visiting competencies. Yes, we can learn with and from one another, but no one else can make us grow.

Frequently the question emerges, "Do we go by ourselves, or do we visit two-by-two?" For the most part, consider visiting singly. Your visit will be more focused and you'll be more helpful. Your visits will be shorter and you'll get to visit with more people.

Yet it makes sense to go as a team on occasion. We visit two-by-two to learn together. Visit with your team partner and with others who will help you grow. Ask if you can go on one or several visits with them. It's not that you begin visiting by going with someone and then head off on your own. Rather, from time to time visit with someone so the two of you can share fun and can learn together.

Sometimes it makes sense to visit two-by-two for security reasons. I have visited in neighborhoods where it would have been safer to visit six-by-six! In some rough neighborhoods, it will be wiser to visit as a two-person team. Should you ever feel that a home or work visit poses a concern for your security, invite someone to go with you.

At the same time, be aware that a visit from two people can be intimidating and overpowering. In most cases, two people at the door or in the workplace is one too many. It's a two-on-one situation. It is particularly intimidating to those who are not currently active in a congregation. You'll be more effective one-on-one, where an equality of relationship is possible.

A two-person visiting team also takes longer than one person, simply in terms of the conversation, even though only one may take the lead. In most cases, you'll be of greater help when you visit singly. One person who knows what he or she is doing can touch the lives of many through visiting. A second person who knows what he or she is doing can also touch the lives of many. When two experienced visitors team up, they cut in half the number of people who can be helped on behalf of God's mission.

Feel free to go two-by-two when you are learning or teaching or for security reasons. Feel free, beyond that, to do excellent visiting on behalf of God's mission one-on-one. Grow yourself forward, and you'll reach many people in the name of Christ.

12:

Suggestions for Visiting

Visiting is a pilgrimage with people. It is not a matter of programs and policies, information and indoctrination, institutions and organizations. Visiting is one person reaching out to another in the name of Christ. This chapter offers some concrete suggestions about how to conduct a successful visit—what to say, when to leave, how to follow up, and so forth—as you venture forth on this pilgrimage.

DETERMINING THE PURPOSE

First, decide the purposes of your visit. There is an old saying, "Plan your day, or the day will plan you." In the same way, plan your visit, or the visit will plan you. It is better to be proactive than simply to react to whatever the other person says. You can still be open and flexible, creative and imaginative. At the same time, be clear in your mind about what you hope to accomplish in this specific visit.

Feel free to have two to four purposes for any visiting contact. Two is sufficient for a constructive, healthy contact. More than four is too many. Some people try to accomplish too much in one visit.

For example, on the first visit you might focus on these purposes:

- names
- mutual interests
- the person's strengths
- beginnings

This may seem obvious, but it is important to learn one another's *names*. Be sure you know the names of the persons you're visiting, and share your name once, twice, or three times, so they learn well who is visiting with them.

Discover something you have in common at the deepest possible levels. Some may discover they have a *mutual* love for fishing, quilting, sports, or baking. People begin to draw toward one another as they discover something they have in common.

Look for the *strengths*, gifts, and competencies of the person you're visiting. Don't go looking for their problems, needs, concerns, weaknesses, and shortcomings. Those may or may not emerge in due course. Go looking for the strengths. Help them to teach you what they do best. Given half a chance, people will share in terms of what they do well. At some future point, they may indeed share with you a problem or a need. The way forward is to build on the residual strengths, however modest, you discovered in the first visit.

Begin a sharing and caring relationship. The purpose of a first visit is to begin a relationship. With newcomers, for example, share the gift of welcoming. The simple purpose of a first visit is to begin.

INITIAL CONTACT

The initial focus of a constructive, healthy visit includes

- the first statement
- the first three minutes

The *first statement* sets up the first three minutes. In your first statement, share who you are, who you are with, and why you are there. Use your own words. Communicate in the first statement a sense of caring, welcoming, inviting, or belonging. With newcomers, a helpful first statement is,

"I'm Bill Freeman with Pleasant Valley congregation. Welcome. We are glad you're part of the community."

Less helpful is a statement like,

"I have come by to bring you some information on the history and programs of our church."

Even less helpful is,

"I hope I'm not being an inconvenience and an interruption."

With that statement you have just taught the person to focus on whether or not you are an interruption, an inconvenience. Don't apologize for being there. The first statement suggested is relational and person-centered. The other two are functional. How you begin teaches people where you are headed.

The *first three minutes* set up the remainder of the visit. These initial minutes teach the person why you are there. People respond well when you have a genuine purpose. Set forth honestly, compassionately, and hopefully why you are there. Keep the first three minutes focused on the direction, content, hopes, and limits you have for the visit.

The first statement provides the initial purpose for the visit. The first three minutes reconfirm and put solidly in place why you are there. When the first statement and the first three minutes contradict—you start with a relational statement but quickly turn to "church talk"—the person being visited will conclude that you don't know why you have come. People do respond to visitors who have a clear purpose as to why they are there.

WHAT NOT TO DO

There are several things not to do when visiting—particularly in a first visit. People are self-conscious enough in a first visit.

The first thing to avoid is *information getting*, such as, "Where were you born, and what has happened since?" Do not turn the visit into a series of interrogations, where you ask a question and they answer, you ask and they answer. Respect their privacy. Avoid questions like,

> "Where were you born?"
>
> "What did your parents do?"
>
> "When did you move here?"
>
> "Where do you work?"
>
> "What kinds of activities do you enjoy?"
>
> "What are the ages of your children?"

Every question increases their self-consciousness and runs the risk of putting them on the defensive.

Imagine you have three hundred-dollar bills in your pocket. Each time you ask a question, you tear up one of these bills. Allow yourself no more than three questions during the course of a visit. More than three questions makes the visit seem like a one-way interrogative session.

If you would like to know something about the person, share something about yourself. If you would like to know something about their family and children, share something about your family and your children. People reciprocate.

I encourage you to use invitational statements. For example, you might gently say,

"Share with me something about yourself."

"Share with me something about your family."

These are statements of an invitational character. They do not have a question mark at the end. And even then, limit the number of invitational statements you are sharing. Remember: The purpose of the visit is not information getting.

The second thing to avoid is *information giving*. Some people take too many brochures and pamphlets on all the church's activities. They provide more information than is wanted.

Information giving about the history of your church is particularly unhelpful. New people cannot participate in your congregation's past. They can participate only in your future. When you focus on your past, you are simply teaching people that it will be a long time before they will ever feel a part of your church.

When you want to share some literature, send it after the visit. For example, you may discover during the visit that there is a preschool child in the family. Feel free to mail them information about your congregation's preschool weekday program. Their receiving the brochure in the mail will be yet another visiting contact. Your personal note on the front of the brochure, "Glad we could visit together," will help. Focus the visit on the person, not on pamphlets, programs, brochures, and bulletins. Feel free to mail any literature that would be a helpful follow-up gesture.

The third thing not to do is *membership hustling*. Some denominations are so preoccupied with membership growth (or stopping the decline) that they create pastors and key leaders preoccupied with it. That, in turn, creates teams who go out and try to get new members. As I survey the history of the Christian movement, I discover again and again that it has been at its best when it focuses on helping

people with their lives and destinies in the name of Christ.
The movement has never done as well when it tries to get
members.

Jesus' invitation to Ananais to go and visit Saul was not
an invitation to go and get him to become a member. There
were no conditions. The visit was to help Saul with his life.

The fourth thing not to do is *salvation scalp hunting.* We
visit to help people with their lives and destinies in the name
of Christ. It is not we who bring salvation. People discover
the saving grace of God and decide to move toward new life.
This is God's work, not ours.

We're not there to push or prod the person toward salvation. We're there to share the grace and love of God. We're
there to share the spirit of compassion and the sense of
community that people discover in Christ.

Our task is invitational, not authoritarian. Invite, don't
push. Remember well how God has shared his grace with
you. Consider the joy, hope, confidence, and assurance you
know as you have sensed the grace of God in your life. Go
and do likewise. Go and share love—and the grace of God.

CLOSING AND LEAVING

Close your visit simply. Avoid closing your visit in an awk-
ward, artificial way. Try not to close and then close your visit
again and then close your visit yet another time. When you
have accomplished the purposes with which you began,
close the visit. Do it graciously and straightforwardly. When
you leave, leave well. Leave in such a spirit that both of you
can look forward to when you might share together again.
End the visit by focusing on them. Do not give an excuse
for leaving. Above all, do not say,

> "Well, I guess I had better be going. I have someone
> else to visit as well."

It is much more helpful to say,

"John and Mary, I have enjoyed our visit together. I look forward to our visiting again. It's been good to be with you."

Then leave. Regrettably, many people do well with the initial stage of the visit and then stumble on the closing and leaving. Close simply. Leave graciously.

When you leave before people are ready for you to leave, they are more likely to share with you what is genuinely troubling them as you head to the door. It is more likely to happen then than at any other time during the visit.

People take an indirect comfort and assurance from the presence of a helping person visiting with them. But when we stay too long, they have absorbed plenty of indirect comfort. They're beginning to wonder how much longer we're going to stay. Leaving the visit soon enough interrupts the indirect comfort and assurance you have been sharing. And it is precisely at this point that people frequently share what is genuinely troubling them in their life's pilgrimage.

When that happens, you have four choices:

1. You can stand and visit about what is troubling them.

2. You can work out a time when you can get together to discuss it more fully.

3. You can go back and sit down and discuss.

4. You can refer them to a resource person who can help in the area that is troubling them.

Use your own wisdom. You don't need to take their troubles on yourself. You might refer them. The basic point is, leave before people are ready for you to go.

Jesus shared three years with his chosen disciples. Consider the grace and patience, the wisdom and thought-

fulness, with which Christ shared with his disciples—and
has shared with us in our own lives.

We might have the grace and patience, wisdom and
compassion, to begin a sharing and caring relationship in a
first visit. Then give the relationship the possibility of growing. Life is a pilgrimage. Visiting is a pilgrimage. Do both
well in the name of Christ.

FOLLOW-UP

The follow-up does not automatically need to be a personal
visit. Share the first visit if you do nothing else. Don't let
the idea of a series of follow-up visits overwhelm you. Some
people never make the first visit; they think it will obligate
them to go back for a second, a third, a fourth visit. The first
visit with the best timing is equal to three to five visits at any
other time.

Your follow-up can happen in several ways. After your
first visit you can

- honor their capacity to follow up
- share a personal note
- make a phone call
- send a direct-mail invitation

One of the best ways is to *honor their capacity to follow
up*. As you leave, you can genuinely and helpfully say to a
person,

"As we can be helpful, we look forward to doing so."

Honor the possibility of their taking the next step. Yet
this is not an excuse for you to do no follow-up.

By the same token, we want to create healthy, whole,
constructive relationships with persons. We don't want to

create codependent relationships. Sometimes the best thing to do is to leave the initiative with them to do the follow-up.

A second way is with a one- or two-sentence *personal note:*

Dear John and Mary,

Glad we could visit together.
As I can be helpful, I look forward to doing so.

Yours,
Jim Wood

The personal note is a simple, thoughtful gesture that helps people to know they are in your prayers and you do care. Send the note within two or three days of the visit.

A third way is with a *phone call.*

"Glad we could visit together. Hope things are going well with you. As I can be helpful, I look forward to doing so."

Or you can conclude your follow-up phone call by inviting them to a major community Sunday or a special event you know would be helpful in their lives. Share the personal phone call within a week or two.

A fourth way is with a *direct-mail invitation.* You have had an excellent visit with them. You have discovered that they have interests in specific areas of your congregation's mission. A direct-mail invitation to a special event or a major community Sunday that relates to their life situation is an excellent way to maintain contact.

Follow up all your visits within one week to one month. That way your visit will still be fresh in their minds. This will constructively reinforce an excellent visit.

These are four possibilities for follow-up. I haven't said much about the specific steps of a follow-up visit. There are three good reasons for this:

- the key visit is the first visit; focus your energies here
- one visit may be sufficient to be helpful
- what happens beyond a first visit is best discovered after the first visit has happened

Sometimes I am asked, "Who does the follow-up?" The answer is, it could be you, or it could be someone else—whoever is a good match. After visiting with a newcomer family, you might know of someone especially well matched with them. Encourage them to be in contact with the newcomer family.

Try not to get so caught up in organizing that you never deliver the follow-up. Let your intent be to do a simple, thoughtful follow-up. Do it well and graciously. God will bless your work.

13:

Excellent Sprinters, Solid Marathon Runners

VALUE YOUR DISTINCTIVE WAY

Visit in whatever way matches the way you do most things. Don't try to base your visiting style on someone else's pattern. Grow your gifts for visiting in the way that works best for you.

Some people are excellent sprinters. They have strong bursts of energy. They do most everything with high intensity and are good at short-term projects and immediate needs. Sprinting is their organizing principle.

Others, by contrast, are solid marathon runners. They maintain a steady, consistent pace as their organizing principle. They like a regular, even routine of ongoing, week-by-week involvement.

Excellent visiting can be done by both sprinters and marathon runners. Both have unique contributions to make. This book builds on the best strengths and competencies of *both* excellent sprinters and solid marathon runners.

Many of the people I've had the privilege of working with are excellent sprinters. Sometimes, from the perspective of a solid marathon runner, excellent sprinters seem to procrastinate.

But they do not procrastinate. As a matter of fact, many people do everything they do in short-term, high-energy bursts near the time at hand. This is the rhythm of life that works best for them.

Regrettably, many visiting programs in the past were designed by persons who were more like solid marathon runners. They were based on this premise:

> Let's all meet every Wednesday (or Monday or Tuesday) night at the church, have a time of fellowship, then go out and visit.
>
> We will do this every Wednesday night—forever and ever, Amen—fifty weeks of the year, year in and year out.
>
> All people who are faithful and committed to the church will join us every Wednesday.

This is the visiting plan of a solid marathon runner for whom weekly visiting works well. Its week-by-week thrust soon loses the interest of excellent sprinters. In fact, one of the primary reasons some people drop out of visiting is because they are excellent sprinters tied into a visiting program that was designed for solid marathon runners, usually by solid marathon runners. People drop out not because they have lost interest but because the program's style is wrong for them. As excellent sprinters, they participate in sprinting fashion. From time to time they come on board in highly intensive, short-term ways. Then they stop participating.

It is not that they lack commitment. It is not that they have shallow faith. They do have a deep commitment. They do have a strong faith. They express it in hundred-yard dashes, not in twenty-six mile marathon runs. There is a diversity of gifts, and God has given many Christians the gift of being excellent sprinters.

God blesses solid marathon runners as well as excellent sprinters. God invites both to share in the mission. The best visiting outreaches value the contributions of both.

I encourage you to develop your strengths as an excellent sprinter or as a solid marathon runner. Do your visiting in the way that suits you best. Have both types on your visiting teams.

There is a mix of these strengths in all of us. At the same time, there is a tendency for one of these to be predominant at a given point in one's life pilgrimage. No one is locked into one or the other. Build your visiting outreach with the gifts, strengths, and competencies of both.

KEY LEADERS

Those who visit are among the key leaders of a congregation. Because we live in an age of mission, the people who participate in the important mission of visiting are the key leaders. In the churched culture of the past, when many people sought out the church on their own initiative, congregations could afford the luxury of asking some of their best leaders to serve on the finance committee or as trustees. Indeed, the statement "We'd better check with the finance committee before we decide on that" was really better understood as "We'd better check with some of our very best leaders before we decide on that."

In a churched culture, churches focused on maintenance, membership, money. It was said that successful congregations had three things: location, location, location. The focus could be on the site, the facilities, and the *inside*. People were coming.

In the mission field, mission congregations do three things in their community: visit, visit, visit. The wise congregation invites some of its best leaders to serve on its visiting teams. With mission congregations, the statement is frequently made, "We'd better check with our visiting teams before we decide on that." Translation: "We'd better check with some of our key leaders before we decide on that" or "We'd better check on how this decision will help our mission with persons in the community."

In mission congregations, decisions are based on how they advance and nurture the mission, not primarily on how they affect the money, space, and facilities. The value system revolves around the mission, not around the maintenance. The key leaders are the persons who lead the mission. The supporting leaders are the ones who care for the maintenance.

Many mission congregations have mission leaders who develop a simple plan for visiting in the community. You will find suggestions about this in the chapters that follow. If your congregation does not yet do visiting in your community, you need not wait on it. Begin with yourself. Be a key leader in the mission.

Today take these steps:

1. Discover the persons whom God is inviting you to visit.

2. Choose your ways of visiting.

3. Decide on the best timing.

4. Grow your gifts for visiting.

5. Build your mission.

Run with compassion. Have fun. Visit with hope. Begin.

Building Your Mission

14:

Your Visiting Outreach

PROGRESS

Wisdom rejoices in progress. Wisdom avoids perfectionism.

I encourage you to advance your visiting purposefully throughout the coming four years. Does it need to look like perfectionism? Certainly not. Will you be moving in the right direction? Yes!

Using your own good judgment, you can set a few visiting objectives for yourself that

- are specific and measurable
- are realistic and achievable
- reinforce one another
- have solid time horizons
- develop the momentum and dynamic of your visiting

The art is progress, not perfectionism.

Set a few objectives, to be accomplished with pace and patience. Develop solid time lines that advance your visiting in the community. Don't set too many objectives, too high, to be accomplished too soon. When we do that, we usually postpone action. Keep your objectives realistic and achievable. Some people berate themselves because they're always "putting things off." The *real* problem is probably not procrastination. The real problem is probably that old friend, the compulsion toward perfectionism.

When we have unrealistic objectives, we know we have set ourselves up to fail. We don't want to fail. We prefer to succeed. When we postpone action, what we are really trying to do is postpone failure.

Many well-intentioned visiting outreaches never get off the ground for that reason. Perfectionism slips into the planning. It causes us to spend too much time in organizational meetings, trying to plan everything so it will be just right. Focus instead on progress.

A FAST BREAK

Look four years ahead. Create a few excellent visiting outreaches. These will become self-generating strengths of your congregation's mission. Do a few key things well. Don't try to do everything.

Invite a few people to become a team to visit with specific persons in your community. Do your visiting for a short period, then rest. No one is asked to visit week in and week out across a full year. In the following possibilities, I describe teams made up of four persons. Each person on the team visits singly. They do pair up as team partners to share resources and to learn from each other. All four may gather, on occasion, for good fun and learning.

You may want to have more or fewer than four persons on a team. It depends on the number of people you look forward to visiting. I use four for these reasons:

- to illustrate the power of what four persons can achieve in visiting

- you are likely to strengthen your own visiting competencies best as you share, from time to time, with three others who are visiting in the same community

The following possibilities are designed for excellent sprinters. They help people to visit for short periods of time and provide generous times for rest, reflection, and prayer in between. Solid marathon runners will find these suggestions helpful as well.

Be sure to arrange your visiting to allow times for rest, prayer, and the fun of looking forward to your next visit. Tired visitors share challenge and commitment, doom and gloom. Rested visitors share compassion and community, cheerfulness and joy. These possibilities focus on doing a few key things well. Not everything will get done. That's fine. This is no place for compulsiveness. We build our strengths in visiting one day at a time, one year at a time.

FIRST-TIME WORSHIPERS

You might feel led to visit with first-time worshipers. Invite three other persons with similar longings to join you on a team. You can visit on

- your congregation's major community Sundays
- a monthly rotation
- a weekly rotation

With the first option, if you have ten such Sundays a year, you would visit on each of those ten Sundays. During the other forty-two Sundays of the year, you can rest, pray, and have fun looking forward to your next visits.

This option works well in congregations where the largest number of first-time worshipers come on the major community Sundays. Yes, there may be some first-time worshipers on other Sundays. No, we would not let perfectionism get to us. We would keep our focus on our ten major community Sundays. Visit your first-time worshipers in whatever way you are led to. Focus on progress, not perfectionism. With some, you might share a personal note. With some, a personal phone call. With some, a personal visit. Focus on *some* contact rather than trying to visit with everyone personally in their homes.

With a monthly rotation, your team can rotate the visiting monthly. Four persons might take turns visiting from one month to the next, as shown on the schedule presented in table 14.1.

Table 14.1 A Monthly Rotation of Visiting with First-Time Worshipers

January	February	March	April
May	June	July	August
September	October	November	December
Orville	*Mary*	*Harold*	*Wilma*

Throughout the year each person has the fun of visiting during three specific one-month periods and has three months off in between.

With a weekly rotation, you can rotate your visiting weekly, taking turns from one week to the next, as shown in table 14.2.

Using this schedule, each person visits during one week of each month. The first-time worshipers on the first Sunday of the month are visited by Orville. He then has the rest of the month off. Any first-time worshipers on the second Sunday will receive a visit in some form from Mary, and so on.

Table 14.2 A Weekly Rotation of Visiting with First-Time Worshipers

First Sunday	Second Sunday	Third Sunday	Fourth Sunday
Orville	*Mary*	*Harold*	*Wilma*

NEWCOMERS

You might feel led to visit with newcomers. Invite three other persons who have similar longings to team up with you. The best timing is in the four months when the highest number of move-ins occur in your community, for example, June through September.

Each one of you visits three newcomers each week, any twelve of the seventeen weeks. Each of you has five weeks off; it is vacation time as well. Visit your three persons in whatever way you are led to. In a given week, you might be led to share one personal note and two personal phone calls. In another week you might share one personal phone call and two personal visits. In another week, one personal note and two personal visits.

Four persons, each visiting three newcomers, contact twelve newcomer families in a week. During those four months, four persons visit with 144 newcomer families. These four persons share a remarkable mission.

At the end of the four months, do this: rest, pray, reflect, give thanks to God for the mission God has given you, have the fun of looking forward to visiting with newcomers next June through September.

In June through September of your first year, you might visit newcomers within a given geographical area of your community. A year later, you might have fun welcoming newcomers who are moving into another area.

OCCASIONAL WORSHIPERS

If you feel led to visit with occasional worshipers, find three others who have similar longings to join you as a team. The best timing is February, March, and April, as we head into Easter. Each one of you visit three occasional worshipers each week, any ten of the thirteen weeks. Each of you has three weeks off. Visit your three persons in whatever way you are led to. One week you might share a personal note with one, a personal phone call with one, and a personal visit with one.

In another week you might share two personal notes and one personal phone call. In another week, one personal phone call and two personal visits. Would you try to do three personal visits in a given week? No. It is probably sharing more contact than is necessary, and it sounds like perfectionism. Many occasional worshipers are helped with a personal note or personal phone call.

Four persons, each sharing three visits, contact 12 occasional worshiper families in a week. During the ten weeks out of the thirteen, your team of four persons contacts 120 households. That is an amazing mission.

At the end of April, do this: rest, pray, reflect, give thanks, look forward to visiting with occasional worshipers next February, March, and April.

RELATIONAL PERSONS

If you feel that you would do best visiting relational persons, invite three persons who feel that this is their strength too to be on a team with you. The best timing is October, November, December, as we head into Christmas. Each one of you visits three relational persons each week, ten of the thirteen weeks. Everyone has three weeks off. Visit in whatever ways you feel led to. Four persons, each sharing three contacts, contact 12 households each week. Your four-person team contacts 120 relational families. You are sharing a wonderful mission.

After Christmas, do this: rest, pray, reflect, give thanks, look forward to visiting with relational persons next October, November, and December.

SHORT-TERM TEAMS

You might feel led to visit with one of the other community groupings. The above examples are simply illustrations. You can grow a four-person team to visit with any of the persons in your community. And, again, you don't need to have four people in order to begin. You can begin. You'll find your team as you visit. This is a constructive, self-help approach to visiting. You have you. You have the Lord. Go ahead and start.

Visit short term. As you go, develop a short-term team. Someone will sense the fun and satisfaction you are discovering and will ask you how they can do it too. They'll see the lives who are being helped. You don't need a long-term team that visits weekly year in and year out. You and your team will illustrate how community visiting can be done.

In your congregation, you might develop from one to four short-term teams. If you had four such teams, they might look like the teams shown in table 14.3.

Begin with your team. Other teams will come into being during the course of the coming years. All four teams don't need to be lined up before you start.

14.3 An Example of Four Visiting Teams in a Congregation

First-time Worshipers	Orville	Mary	Harold	Wilma
Newcomers	Gene	Ann	Virginia	Walt
Occasional Worshipers	John	Lynne	Valerie	Nancy
Relational Persons	Glen	Virginia	Joe	Sue

An Example

I encourage you to be more interested in the visiting than in the numbers. I do want you to see, however, what four teams of just four persons each can accomplish in a short time. In each of the four years, first-time worshipers will be visited. And in each of the four years, 144 newcomer families will be welcomed, for a total of 576 families in all.

Beginning in year two, occasional worshipers will be visited, 120 families each year, for three years—360 families in all. Relational persons will be visited with the same strength—360 families.

Because of the visiting of these four short-term teams, first-time worshipers have been visited, plus 1,296 households. A few people who have a love for visiting and are growing in their competencies can touch the lives of many. Each team can come on board in successive time frames, and each will develop a self-renewing, self-resourcing outreach with the community persons they visit.

Whom to Invite

Discover persons with genuine longings and competencies for each team. Help them to see themselves as a visiting team together. I don't mean that they'll do their visiting as a team. I mean that they'll be resources for one another, share new insights with one another, and back up one another as appropriate. Some studies say laypersons are twice as effective in visiting as pastors. Some studies say pastors are twice as effective in visiting as laypersons. The truth: Competent persons are twice as effective as incompetent persons in visiting.

Encourage people in your congregation and your pastor to be part of a short-term visiting team. Lots of people and pastors have competencies for visiting and will enjoy strengthening these gifts. Both will do well, not because one is a layperson or one is a pastor, but because they have a sincere desire to visit on behalf of God's mission and to have fun developing their competencies.

Have this confidence: Many short-term teams discover new visiting team members from among the community persons they visit. The visiting teams become self-renewing and self-resourcing.

Use your own wisdom. Rejoice in progress. Grow your team. Have fun visiting. Move swiftly. Run a fast break. Too many churches spend too much time in the locker room. The game is won on the court.

15:

The Congregation's Witness

POWER AND PRESENCE

Congregations with a strong visiting outreach have a special power and presence. Their power is in their assurance that they are doing what God has called them to do. Their presence is felt in the community—reaching out to people in helpful ways. Their presence is felt in people's lives—helping them to advance their future courses and destinies.

Congregations with this sense of power and this spirit of presence are strong mission congregations of compassion and hope. They contribute greatly to the character and quality of life in the community and help many in the name of Christ.

HELPING FACTORS

Several factors help congregations to develop their visiting. When these helping factors are lacking, the congregation's visiting outreach becomes blocked, which, regrettably, contributes to the withering and eventual demise of this outreach. These helping factors include

- solid secretarial support
- a focused, limited amount of time to be invested in administration
- persons growing their competencies for visiting
- confidence, compassion, and hope

Think about which of these aids are well in place in your congregation and which ones you can put in place in the coming four years.

SECRETARIAL SUPPORT

Focus on people work, not paper work. Strong visiting and excellent secretarial support go together. Wherever the visiting is weak or absent, there is usually either inadequate or a total absence of secretarial support for the visiting outreach.

To say that another way, the first thing that stops getting done when there is inadequate secretarial support is pastoral and lay visiting in the community. Visiting is the first thing that goes out the window.

When there is inadequate secretarial support, someone has to step in to do the secretarial work. For the most part it is you, persons on your visiting teams, and your pastor who have to take on the role of secretary.

There is a range of competencies in secretarial support:

- administrative coordinator
- administrative assistant
- executive secretary
- general secretary
- receptionist

- clerk typist
- typist
- clerk

These are levels of competencies, not titles. Have well in place the competencies of any one of the first three. At any strong mission congregation, I would be happy to meet the pastor. At any successful business, I would be happy to meet the president. And at either place I would want also to meet the administrative coordinator, administrative assistant, or executive secretary. That is the person who administratively sees that everything gets done—on time and in good order.

This is the person who glues the work together week by week and who knows what needs to be done next. Before anyone else has even thought of it, it has been completed and is on the desk ready for signature. I have an extraordinary appreciation for competent administrative coordinators, administrative assistants, and executive secretaries.

The clerk typist is the one who doesn't know what needs to be done next and who sits and waits for instructions before doing anything. The clerk typist does know clerking and typing, but it is the clerk typist who can become the ball and chain to pastors, quickly teaching them that it isn't safe to leave the office and go visiting.

Why? Because whenever the pastor is gone, either the wrong things get done, the right things get done the wrong way, or nothing much gets done. The clerk typist is quite dependent on the resources of another person who has the skills of an administrative coordinator, administrative assistant, or executive secretary.

One of the most significant helping factors is to deliver excellent secretarial support to yourself, your visiting teams, and your pastor. This secretarial support could be volunteer, part-time, or full-time. Whether volunteer or paid, the key distinction is professional excellence.

This person will

- help to discover names of community persons
- provide names to you and your visiting team
- develop a simple system of notes and follow-up dates

Then your primary focus can be visiting. Lack of competent secretarial support impedes visiting. Visiting teams end up spending too much time sorting cards, thinking through who should visit whom, and organizing the sequence of the visits. They spend their time doing secretarial tasks and have less time to visit. With excellent secretarial support, the visiting teams and the pastor simply go and visit.

One congregation asked if I thought they should add more secretarial support. I had been there several days as their consultant and had seen who did most of the executive secretarial work. The church staff consisted of a pastor, an associate pastor, and a clerk typist. The consequence was that the pastor and associate pastor had become the executive secretaries, and the clerk typist did what she was asked to do.

The key leaders asked what would help. I suggested to them that they already had too many secretaries. Both the pastor and the associate pastor were doing too much paperwork. They needed either to hire an excellent executive secretary or to help their clerk typist quickly acquire the competencies of one. Then the two pastors could stop being executive secretaries and focus on the visiting.

To be sure, when you have a pastor whose best gifts lie in administration, you may want a shepherding secretary who provides a balance. When I discover a pastor whose best competencies are in administration, I encourage that pastor to do what he or she does well—namely, administration. And in that instance, that pastor will probably invest more than twelve hours a week in administrative duties because of this personal capability.

By the same token, when you have a pastor whose gifts are in visiting, it is more helpful to have, at the very least, an executive secretary who frees the pastor and visiting teams to exercise their best gifts. It is less helpful to have a clerk typist who does not deliver the administrative work yet who is always on the phone "counseling" persons in the congregation.

An excellent executive secretary will virtually double the effectiveness of a visiting pastor and visiting teams. It is this person who helps them to have the time to do what they do best—visiting in the community. By contrast, the clerk typist who is not getting the administrative secretarial work done helps neither the office work nor the visiting mission.

LIMITED TIME FOR ADMINISTRATION

Help yourself, your key leaders, and your pastor focus on people work, not administrative work. A visiting outreach is strengthened when key leaders and pastors develop the practice of investing focused, limited amounts of time in administration. Runaway administration can block the growth of a visiting mission, miring key leaders and pastors in committee meetings, paperwork, and office details.

Merrill Douglass, a lifelong friend of mine, is one of the leading time management consultants in the country. He developed what is known as "Douglass's Law of Clutter." Think of a desk, piled high with stacks and stacks of papers, a pile and a mess. Douglass's Law of Clutter states, "Clutter expands to fill the space available."

One of my friends had a desk piled so high with stacks of papers that he could hardly see the desk. His solution was to get another desk. Now he has two desks—piled high with stacks and stacks of papers. Clutter does expand to fill the space available.

Callahan's Principle of Administration states, *"Administration expands to fill the time available."*

Some studies have found that many pastors invest 57 percent of their time in administration. Most pastors originally felt called to the mission; then they discovered themselves forced into doing administration. No wonder we have pastors with depression, despair, and despondency.

Administration does expand to fill the time available. To control it, we must limit the time available.

I have spent considerable energy, effort, research, and teaching in the field of administration and finance. I encourage pastors to invest *no more than* eight to twelve hours a week in

- administration
- committee meetings
- administrative detail
- paperwork

Some pastors are surprised at this suggestion. They expect a teacher of administration to suggest that they spend more time administering—as though it were of vital, central importance to the mission. As a matter of fact, for the sake of the mission, it is important that pastors limit themselves to no more than eight to twelve hours a week in the combination of the four endeavors listed above.

The more time spent in meetings, the less time spent in visiting. When some pastors say they don't have time for visiting, they're really saying they haven't yet learned how to control the time they spend in administration. The result is, therefore, that they limit the time they spend visiting.

Time spent visiting, helping people with their lives and destinies, is more important, more satisfying. Time spent in meetings is usually less important and is definitely less satisfying. If they have figured out how to limit the more satisfying time for visiting, they can surely figure out how to limit the less satisfying administrative and meeting time.

I can find nowhere in the Bible where it says, "Be ye therefore on a committee, and blessed will be your reward in heaven." I can find nothing in the Bible that says, "Blessed are you who sit in long, weary committee meetings night after night in your local church."

What I do find in the Bible is the invitation "Go." What I do find in the Bible again and again is our Lord's invitation to go into the world and help persons with their lives and destinies in the name of Christ.

Yes, key leaders and pastors may give up some meetings. Yes, they may have shorter meetings. Yes, they may meet only as necessary.

What is called for is a culture of visiting in the community. We have, regrettably, developed a culture of committees in our churches.

In our time God invites pastors and key leaders to be missionary pastors and mission leaders, not professional ministers and committee leaders. As people discover this central calling, we will find it most helpful—and possible—to focus limited time on administrative work.

DEVELOPING GIFTS AND COMPETENCIES

A central helping factor to growing strong visiting outreach in the community is having people who are growing their gifts and competencies for visiting. This is done in large part by focusing on your strengths, not your weaknesses.

Visiting is a matter of wisdom, judgment, vision, common sense, and prayer. Visiting cannot be reduced to data and demographics, graphs and charts. Visiting is not a matter of gimmicks and gadgets. Visiting is a matter of persons who have a genuine spirit of compassion and a strong sense of community.

One learns visiting by doing visiting. When we reach out to persons in the community in the name of Christ, we will make our fair share of mistakes, and we will thereby learn, discover, and grow as we move forward in visiting. We enhance our initial strengths by practicing those strengths.

We don't need to know everything there is to know about visiting before we begin. Visiting is a matter not so much of information and knowledge as of compassion and mission. It is a matter of having a deep longing to reach out to people in the name of Christ.

Whatever anxieties and fears we might have, they will not be overcome by tricks and fads. They will be overcome by the profound longings we have to reach out to people. They will be overcome by the sense that God is sending us to help persons in the community. To be sure, one of the obstacles in some congregations is that there appear to be no persons who have the competencies for visiting. Look more carefully. You'll find that congregations have many persons with the strengths and gifts for visiting in your community, and these people have the capacity to grow their gifts.

More often than not, the real blocking factor is that we have asked those persons to serve elsewhere—on committees inside the church, to fill slots in an organizational chart. We have deployed into administrative areas the people who would do the best visiting.

The way forward is to revise the organizational chart. Develop a mission-driven congregation. When the nominating group meets, help them to have as their first two priorities

- nominating the best possible persons to the teams who visit in the community
- keeping those who are already visiting on their visiting teams rather than pulling them away to some committee

Then fill in the administrative positions and functions in appropriate ways.

In this way, you'll help people share their best strengths on behalf of God's mission. In turn, they will be sharing the mission in the community. You'll be matching the plays with the players. You'll be sending in the plays that the players can run. There are more people in a local congregation who have a gift for visiting than there are those who have a gift for administration.

When we establish an organizational structure that matches the strengths, gifts, and competencies of people in the congregation, when we fill the visiting and mission teams first, then we will have put in place an amazing helping factor for visiting. What administration that needs getting done will still get done.

CONFIDENT HOPE, STRONG COMPASSION

Another helping factor is visiting teams who have a confident hope in the future and deep compassion for persons in the community. By contrast, one of the blocking factors for visiting is fear and a desire for safety and security.

I often wondered why pastors and congregations spent so much time in committee meetings. It finally dawned on me that one of the reasons is fear of failure and a desire for safety. Committee meetings are safer than visiting in the community.

Now, to be sure, in our committee meetings we have our own fusses and feuds. At the same time, by comparison, these church meetings pose less risk than visiting with persons about their lives and destinies. In committee meetings we mostly talk about simpler, pleasant things. In visiting we discover profound human hurts and hopes that challenge us to have hope and compassion, that invite our own growth.

It is more troubling to be in the world than it is to remain inside the church. I honor this. There are times when we all long for the security of committee meetings that have pleasant conversations and, on occasion, wranglings over incidentals. We long for the quick-closure, short-term-result activities inside the church.

What helps us to visit in the community is the confident hope that God goes before us, that God is working in the lives of those we visit. What helps us to leave the locker room and play the game on the field is our strong passion to help people. The richness of helping persons in the name of Christ encourages us to give away our need for security and to go forth into the community.

Make sure you have excellent secretarial support. Invest focused, limited time in administration. Deploy well those who have gifts, strengths, and competencies for visiting. Have a confident hope and strong compassion. These helping factors will give your visiting outreach power and presence in the community.

16:

The Pastor Visits

VISITING AND PREACHING

Visiting advances preaching. There is a direct correlation between the two. The more visiting the pastor does, the stronger his or her preaching.

There are two reasons for this. (1) The preaching is in touch with the lives of those in the community and the congregation. (2) The people know their pastor loves and lives with them. Without this, the preaching will be less in touch with people's lives, and they won't usually sense a mutual bond of love.

The difference is in the visiting more than the preaching.

One church is among the largest in its denomination. Were you and I to hear the pastor preach, we'd see that he almost whispers the sermon, in a halting fashion. From an objective point of view, we might rate him a 5 on a scale of 1 to 10.

That pastor is the legendary shepherd in the community—not just within the congregation but in the community. Year in and year out, the people who are gathered in that congregation each Sunday morning hear the preaching and shepherding wisdom of a beloved pastor. From their perspective, the preaching rates a 9 or a 10. There are many congregations—small, medium, and large—where that same thing happens every Sunday. Sometimes when you want to improve the preaching, you improve the visiting.

MUTUAL TRUST, RESPECT, INTEGRITY

Visiting advances mutual trust, respect, and integrity between the community and the congregation. The visiting of a pastor and key leaders helps to grow that relationship with your community.

Often this relationship has developed between the key leaders and the pastor. They have invested considerable time together in activities and committee meetings. They see one another a great deal. There are long meetings, rich discussions. Sometimes this relationship of mutual trust does not develop so well between the key leaders/the pastor, on the one hand, and the grassroots of the congregation, on the other hand. Moreover, a larger gap frequently exists between the key leaders/the pastor and persons in the community. The key leaders and the pastor often become so busy among themselves that they lose touch with the grassroots and the community.

While there is an increased interest in religion in our time, there is a decreased interest in church. We've neglected the community too long. We've counted on the community to come to us.

Nothing in the Bible suggests that our Lord expected that the community would come to us. We are the ones to go out into the community. We are the ones who can help transform it. We are the ones to invite people to new life in Christ.

We can form a bridge to the increased interest in religion as we develop an increased interest in the community.

As we improve the quality of our visiting outreach, we advance the mutual trust, respect, and integrity between the church and the community.

SHEPHERDING, ADMINISTRATION, AND BICKERING

Visit more and you will bicker less. There is a direct relationship:

> The more visiting, the less bickering.
>
> The less visiting, the more bickering.

Some congregations bicker a lot among themselves. Frequently this correlates with a lack of visiting and can last for years.

Some business management experts advocate MBWA—Management by Walking Around. Managers leave their regional offices and visit among the workers in the stores. They leave their offices and visit among the workers on the factory floor.

Too many key leaders and pastors spend too much time in committee meetings inside. The factory floor is the community. The factory floor is not the church building. The art is to be walking around in the community, not inside the church. People who live in the community are helped by a shepherding visit. Yes, some of the people who live in the community are also in the congregation. But it is shortsighted to say, "We must take care of our own first before we do anything else." Jesus didn't teach the disciples to "take care of yourselves before you do anything else." Jesus didn't instruct the disciples to first visit among themselves.

Jesus invited the disciples to be out in the world. When you visit in the world, you will also visit persons in your congregation. When you limit yourself to visiting only people in the congregation or say that this must be done first, that will help neither your congregation nor your community.

The concept that we must take care of our own first misses who "our own" really are. People in the community are "our own." God's family includes all of them. God's love is for the world. When we visit in the community, we are sharing with people of whom God thinks a great deal.

Share the richness of your visiting in the community. The bickering in the community and in the congregation will be less. You'll learn to love one another more fully, to grow together more graciously and gratefully. Visiting contributes to the character and quality of life in your community.

MISSION VISITING

We now live in one of the richest ages for mission the Christian movement has ever seen. On a mission field, the basic principle of visiting and preaching is this: *Spend one hour in visiting for each minute you preach.*

Fortunately, some sermons will be shorter.

Don't take the principle so literally that you carry a stopwatch to measure elapsed time during visiting. Contrast it with a principle mentioned during the churched culture of the 1940s and 1950s. That principle said, Spend one hour in preparation for each minute you preach.

Where the following four conditions could be met, pastors could invest one hour of preparation for each minute they preached: (1) Most important, there was a churched culture. People were seeking out the church on their own initiative. All the church had to do was wait for them to show up. (2) It was a well-established church in a large city. (3) It worked best where there was a large, multiple staff who did most of the rest of the work. The pastor was thereby freed to focus on the sermon. (4) The purpose of the sermons was both to be helpful in people's lives and to be published in books.

Where the following four conditions are true, I encourage pastors to invest one hour in visiting for each minute they preach: (1) Most important, there is an unchurched culture, where people are no longer seeking us out on their own initiative. (2) Whether the church is in a large city, a town, a village, or a rural area, the congregation is a strong mission outpost. (3) There is no large staff to do most of the rest of the work. (4) The preaching is primarily to be helpful in people's lives and destinies, and the sermons will not necessarily be published in books.

Where these four things are true, I encourage pastors to spend one hour in visiting for each minute they preach. Each hour spent in visiting *is*, in fact, an hour spent in sermon preparation—from a missionary perspective. Some pastors have responded to this advice with concern. If they're going to do a twenty-minute sermon, they ask where they are going to find twenty hours for visiting. Two suggestions help.

First, it is helpful to be reminded that the person who advocated the earlier principle—spend one hour in sermon preparation for each minute you preach—was also known to have said that when he quit visiting for several months, he almost ran out of things to preach about. Visiting helped with his preparation for preaching, and thoughtful pastors are deeply interested in preparing for their sermons.

Second, I encourage pastors to focus on the *spirit* of the principle. Don't worry about where you can find exactly one hour to visit for exactly each minute you preach. You may not in fact achieve that. That's fine. It's the spirit of the principle that will help you. Don't turn the principle into some new legalism. Just as pastors set aside regular time for sermon preparation, they can set aside time for community visiting. The visiting might take place in an excellent sprinter, short-term way or in a solid marathon runner way.

Sometimes the regular time set aside for sermon preparation and the time set aside for visiting in the community crowd out a committee meeting. I encourage pastors to be at peace; go visit. Be a visiting pastor, not an administrator.

Yes, there are some committee meetings that a pastor does well to attend. Usually a thoughtful conversation by phone or in person with the chair of the committee helps greatly. Most pastors have felt called to be shepherds and preachers, not administrators. Heed your calling.

Indeed, congregations teach me again and again that what they look for in a pastor is

- a good shepherd
- a good preacher
- a wise, caring leader
- a person with a sense of mission in the community

They do not primarily look for an administrator, a manager, a boss. There are enough of these. They look for a missionary pastor in visiting, preaching, and in compassionate leading.

I developed the principle "Spend one hour in visiting for each one minute you spend preaching" primarily to illustrate a mission point: that principles from a churched culture appropriately come under examination in a mission field.

In a mission field, the pastor's visiting

- advances preaching
- advances mutual trust and respect between the community and the congregation

- lends integrity to the congregation
- helps administration
- reduces bickering

In a mission field, visiting is decisive, so share it and God will bless it.

17:

Sacrament and Cloud

GRACE

A visit is a sign of grace. It is like a sacrament—an outer and visible sign of an inner and spiritual grace. A visit is an act of sharing healing and wholeness. It is a time of joy and wonder. The lives of two persons share grace, compassion, community, hope.

A visit has its own integrity and value. It's neither a sales technique nor a means to an end. We visit as an expression of the incarnation, as a way of sharing the mission.

Visiting is central to the experience of the Christian movement. God himself is a visitor.

Praise to the Lord, the God of Israel, for he has *visited* and redeemed his people. *Luke 1:68*

Sometimes we've become preoccupied with the part of the text that says God has redeemed his people. The text is clear. God is not some distant, far-off, nebulous entity. Our God is the God who has *visited* his people. J. B. Phillips once wrote a play titled *The Visited Planet,* telling of Christ as the greatest visit of all.

God visits to redeem. God visits, then redeems, and not from afar. God's visit with us has a sacramental character, just as ours on behalf of God's mission do. Visiting is the key with which many people open the door to relationship with God, to meaning and hope for their lives.

As a sacramental act, a visit is among the deepest, most visible expressions of grace that people share with one another. One person seeks out another person for the sake of sharing good news. God's grace is present in the visit.

By God's own action, God has shown us that visiting is what he invites us to do. That God has visited his people is an amazing gift. Among all the things God might have done, it is astonishing, extraordinary, unheard of, that God would visit with us.

In going out to share Christ, we discover Christ. Jesus said,

Lo, I am with you always. *Matthew 28:20*

Jesus invites the disciples to *Go*. Then he assures them of his presence with them. It is in the going that we discover the presence of Christ. It is not accidental that the invitation to *Go* occurs first; then the assurance comes. We find Christ in the midst of the world. When we stay "inside," we wither and decay.

Christ wanted the disciples to know where they would find his presence—in the world. Christ wants us to know that in visiting we will discover his compassion and hope, the strength of his presence and assurance, the power of his love and grace.

I'm suggesting that your visit is like sharing a sacrament. You are surrounded by a sacred spirit when you visit. There is a genuine sense in which God is richly and fully present in it.

A visit, finally, is not our own doing. It is a gift of God. We receive as we share. Christ, in his wisdom, knows that the great good news of joy and wonder, compassion and hope, is received as it is shared. If not shared, it wastes away. Christ shares his grace with us in our visiting, and we discover him as we share him.

COMPASSION

A visit is a sign of compassion. Visiting is not a matter of duty or obligation. Please don't go visiting out of a sense of dutiful commitment. You won't be at your best. The visit won't be at its best. You won't be helpful in people's lives.

Those who visit best see a visit as an expression of sharing and caring, love and concern. Through visiting, people share their faith in deeds as well as in words. Compassion sharing is as helpful as faith sharing. Deeds of compassion speak as strongly as words. A visit is a deed of compassion.

People who visit with a compelling sense of compassion are more interested in how they can help than in what words they should say. Their compassion gives them the words that are needed and helps them focus the visit with the person being visited.

Compassion is foundational to healthy relationships. Kids care about what the teacher knows because they know the teacher cares. The team plays well for the coach because they know the coach cares for the team. The family pulls together when there is a genuine spirit of compassion.

Compassion runs. It doesn't wait in the house for the young son to draw nigh. Compassion doesn't walk slowly and begrudgingly toward the young son. Compassion runs.

In Luke 15, verse 20, we discover these words:

And when the young son was yet a long way off, his father saw him and had compassion and he ran to him.

The text does not say, "And while his young son was yet a long way off, the father saw him and waited in the house."

The text does not say, "And while the young son was yet a long way off, the father saw him and walked slowly, begrudgingly."

What the text says is, The father had *compassion* and he *ran* to him.

Compassion runs. Compassion doesn't wait or walk. Compassion is not a matter of waiting for people in your community to show up in church. It is not a matter of slowly, begrudgingly walking to them, as though they should have had an interest and showed up on their own. Compassion runs to persons in the community and shares with them the richness of God's compassion.

God runs to us with compassion. God has shown us how to run with compassion. God invites us to run with compassion.

COMMUNITY

A visit is a sign of community. From ancient times until today, and throughout the planet, an important custom has been the extension of genuine hospitality to strangers. When the stranger approaches and is invited into the campfire circle, the hosts offer an almost sacred welcome. There is the sense that, for this moment, we are community with one another.

When we visit, we express our interest in community. We're not visiting simply to get information or to give information. We're not visiting primarily to get members. In these days of isolation and insulation, of loneliness and despair, we visit to express our solidarity, our sense of community, with one another.

People are desperately searching for community. For many people their sense of community has been broken. Our visits with them are genuine gestures of community. We will visit with people who are scared, scarred, cold, indifferent, angry. What else could one expect in a world where family and community structures have collapsed all around?

As you visit, think of your best friends. You'll be amazed at how many new best friends you'll discover in your visits. Remember also those with whom you have found a sense of community. You'll be amazed at the sense of community you'll both discover and share in your visits.

HOPE

Our hope is in God. Civilizations rise and fall. Empires come and go. The mission of God is eternal. It endures, and it is where our hope lies. A visit is a sign of mission, a sign of hope.

We visit because God first visited us. In the New Testament we discover these words:

We love, because he first loved us. *1 John 4:19*

Christ comes to us. He doesn't wait for us. Christ visits us to share his compassion and hope, and we visit in the same spirit—to share the good news.

The purpose of our visiting is mission growth, not church growth. There are a few who have said that visiting no longer works. But they have in mind that it no longer works to achieve church growth. That misses the point.

The purpose is mission. Visiting works for mission. Visiting may or may not work for membership growth. The point is, in visiting people's lives are helped in the name of Christ. God calls us to a theology of service, not a theology of survival. The purpose of visiting is mission growth, discipleship growth. Someone once asked me, "Is evangelism the answer to church growth?" That is the wrong question.

We're not called to be preoccupied with the survival of an institution. God calls us to be preoccupied with the lives and destinies of persons in the name of Christ.

These are more helpful questions:

- Is visiting the answer to mission growth?
- Is visiting the answer to discipleship growth?
- Do we live out mission and evangelism in our visiting?
- Do people discover compassion and hope in visiting?

The answer to these questions is *Yes*.

God gives his Son freely, without obligation. A gift is a gift when there is no obligation. God visits us that we might discover grace, compassion, community, hope.

The church is called to be *in* the world, but not of the world. The church's identity is *in* the world. Jesus prayed to God,

> As thou didst send me into the world, so I have sent them into the world. *John 17:18*

We visit freely, without obligation. We visit as a gift. A gift with an obligation isn't a gift. We don't visit to obligate people but to offer the gifts of grace, compassion, community, and hope. God shows us the way. We visit because God first visits us, and God is our hope.

CLOUD OF WITNESSES

Our lives are surrounded by a great cloud of witnesses. As we visit, we are surrounded by this cloud of witnesses. The mission of the Christian movement is never individualistic. No one visits alone.

> Therefore, since we are surrounded by so great a cloud of witnesses, . . . let us run with unflinching purpose the race that is set before us, looking unto Jesus. *Hebrews 12:1*

This cloud of witnesses is made up of our mentors, encouragers, nurturers, coaches, cheerleaders, and of all who have visited on behalf of the Christian movement since the time of Christ. They go with us as we visit.

Christ is with you. The disciples are with you. Paul is there with you. The missionaries of the early church, who carried the Christian gospel to the far corners of the world, are there with you. Augustine, Thomas, Francis, Luther, Calvin—these and many more are with you.

Across the centuries, people who have gone visiting have sensed the presence of all these witnesses—known and unknown—with them as they visit. They are there to encourage you; try to sense their presence as you visit.

We don't visit alone. We go in the company of all who have gone before and who will follow—sharing God's compassion and grace, peace and hope, with those in the community. They give us confidence that our visits hold promise for people's lives and destinies.

Throughout the history of Christianity, there have been important times when visiting in the community has been central to the movement. This is one of those times. Go. Visit well in the name of God. Let us run with unflinching purpose the race that is set before us. Look unto Jesus.